MW00604544

THE
CONVERSATION
EDGE

AILEEN GIBB

49 PRACTICES FOR CREATING BETTER CONVERSATIONS IN LIFE AND LEADERSHIP

(A COMPANION BOOK TO *ASKING GREAT QUESTIONS*)

Copyright © 2020 Aileen Gibb
First Edition: January 2020
ISBN: 978-1-7770501-0-8

All rights reserved.

No part of this publication may be reproduced in any form or by any means, electronic or mechanical, including photocopying, recording or any information browsing, storage or retrieval system, without permission in writing from the publisher.

Published by:
Aileen Gibb

Cover Design: Lieve Maas, BrightLightGraphics.com

FOR JAKE

"One of the things that makes us most wonderfully human is our ability to use words to connect. One of the biggest barriers that needs breaking down is the conversation barrier. If we all spent the time to talk to a stranger, speak to a colleague or even chat with our friends and family more, the world would be a brighter place. I know it's simple, but it's true."

— RICHARD BRANSON, 2019

FOREWORD

"Human conversation is the most ancient and easiest way to cultivate the conditions for change — personal change, community and organisational change, planetary change. If we can sit together and talk about what's important to us, we begin to come alive."

— MARGARET J WHEATLEY, from *Turning to One Another*

We *begin* to come alive...

On the day of my 60th birthday, as I worked on the pages of this book, I learned about a research study[1] which showed that people dying of Stage 4 lung cancer relished honest, meaningful conversation. Each day for the rest of their lives, a dedicated palliative care nurse asked them, "What will make today a good day you you?" These conversations — where they felt caregivers truly listened to them — helped the terminal patients live 25% longer, incur lower healthcare costs, and shorten hospital stays, when compared to patients who were not asked that question each day.

The question, and the conversation it generated, appeared to enrich and extend the last days of their lives.

If you're reading this book, I trust you are not facing such a significant edge as your own mortality. You may, however, find that some of your everyday conversations feel almost as scary or painful. *"I'd die if I said/ heard that."*

Yet, this research affirms that life gets better when we are curious enough to ask people what gives them meaning, and when we actually step into that conversation edge with them (as opposed to avoiding conversations that we imagine to be as momentous as the one about dying).

If making time for real conversation might prevent us from getting ill or stressed in the first place, and might make for healthier people, relationships, organisations and society, then why would we wait until we're dying to find out? Why not get much better at our conversations now?

This book of practices will help you do so.

I want it to be as useful to you each day as the palliative care counsellors were for the patients in the study. I want it to be at hand when you need it. I want it to be something you'll reach for and use. I want this book to ask you to make more conscious choices each moment of the day in your conversations and your connections with people.

I don't know if it will save your life, but it might save your relationship, job, project or team. It might save you from embarrassment or fear. It might save you from yourself. If it has any chance to save you in any way, it will require you to play your part by putting these ideas into practice daily.

In this book, you'll find the broader concept of conversation broken down into small, specific practices. I invite you to focus on one practice at a time. The more you practice, the more your conversations will transform; one day it will all come together as you realise you are hearing, seeing, experiencing and benefiting from conversations in ways which had previously escaped you.

You'll find and expand what I'm calling your conversation edge: that moment when you hesitate or pull back from what needs to be said.

Once you go beyond that edge, your world changes.

Now, as my editor pointed out, and since I've lived and traveled extensively on both sides of the pond, I've picked up, dropped, and picked up again the various preferences, spellings and linguistic ticks associated with these places. I like to say I'm "multilingual" and this translates into my writing.

You may come across various spellings or grammatical styles and wonder if I'm writing for a U.K. or a U.S. audience. Since the book is about conversation, I hope you don't feel it matters too much that these styles dance with each other here.

I hope you enjoy the dance, as your conversation moves to a new rhythm in partnership with others.

Aileen

INTRODUCTION
CONVERSATION AS PRACTICE

"A practice may be defined as the dedicated, daily exercise of commitment, will, and focused intention aimed, on one level, at the achievement of mastery in a field. Practice has a space — and that space is sacred."

— STEPHEN PRESSFIELD, from his book, *Turning Pro*

Privileged as I have been with the confidential conversations of my coaching clients for many years, I have come to respect conversation as a form of sacred space that invites devoted practice.

Yet, we rarely attend to conversation as practice. Not in the way many of us approach yoga as a practice that invites daily devotion and commitment in order to expand our bodies and our minds; or in the way music can be a lifelong practice for even the most accomplished musicians; or in the way an athlete commits each day to perfecting the nuances of technique that may lead to the winners podium.

We're much more casual about conversation.

As one leader once commented to me, "I don't have time to do nice conversations with everyone, Aileen." At the time, I failed to step into deeper conversation with him to explore the territory and possibilities of conversations that go beyond coffee room chitchat.

We are natural conversationalists; we can all talk, yet we've become lazy and casual with our words, thoughts, attention and our relationships in a world that values quick answers and truncated responses. It's a world where, as my colleague Gary Diggins once cited, we now rely on technology to convey our messages, and emojis to share our deepest joys and concerns.

In this world, conversations are often incomplete and unsatisfying.

Yearning for deeper, more meaningful and more complete conversation, many people turn to professional coaches, believing they can't have these important conversations in their workplace or their personal life without support. My inspired conversations with people around the world suggest otherwise. My work has taken me from Kazakhstan to Venezuela, across Europe and North America and into Africa. In each of these places, across dozens of cultures, people have responded eagerly when invited into the space for deeper conversations.

In that sacred space, enriched by deep listening, artful questions and mindful respect for each contributor, I've seen conversations inspire new business ideas, save marriages, launch new careers, heal differences, build teams and enrich relationships.

Today's dependence on smart phones and tablets has relegated such meaningful conversation to not-so-close encounters of a third kind. We might as well be aliens talking a different language and not understanding each other.

"The art of conversation is perhaps the most commonly neglected skill on the globe," cites Judy Apps in her book, *The Art of Conversation*. Like any neglected art, it requires that you return to it through attentive practice — one that, in the case of conversation, reminds you what it takes to live fully, with real human-to-human connection as an essential foundation for success.

I ask you: how often do you leave a conversation feeling it wasn't quite complete?

Have you ever wished afterwards that you'd said, done or asked something else? How often do you want to go back and express what you said in a different way? How often do you hold back from saying what was truly on your mind? Have you avoided saying something because you thought it would be uncomfortable for the other person to hear?

How often do your conversations fail to live up to the outcomes you hoped for?

These are the edges you come up against in conversation: those moments when, if even one word had been said or heard differently, the outcome might have changed.

We all have these edges. And times call for us to reclaim them, and discover what's beyond.

It is upon us to be courageous and curious enough to ask deeper questions, to start conversations with strangers and people we are curious to know better, to speak up and use our voices when we have something to say. It is within us to explore new ideas with people who see the world differently from how we look at it, and to connect more meaningfully as real human beings rather than as job titles or generic labels.

I've watched many clients come to their edges in our coaching conversations. At first, they hesitate to explore them. And I've also watched and listened as clients move beyond their edges, and discover themselves anew.

I want this for you too.

I want you, as a leader, to create conversations that bring people to their edges, and to explore beyond them together.

Leading people into the conversations they yearn for will give you an unparalleled edge in today's world, more so than those leaders who think, like the client I mentioned earlier, that conversation is only wasted time being nice with each other.

You may well have read one of the 40,000 or so books on the topic of conversation.

You may have digested various theories and frameworks. Perhaps you've been romanced by those that offer you improved conversations in one evening, or with little effort.

There's a lot of theory, but there's no silver bullet when you're in an actual conversation. So, I've created this book: not of theory or frameworks, but of practices.

I offer you 49 small, bite-size elements taken from the type of conversations that have changed the lives of my coaching clients.

You are invited to practice these one at a time throughout the year. Maybe you'll choose one for a day, or one per week. Go slow with them. Give each practice its due time and attention, so you can build up your skills. Eventually, you'll discover that your conversations are very different from what they used to be.

I urge you to focus on each subtle shift, practice by practice, conversation by conversation. Like persisting with regular yoga, or developing any athletic muscle, you'll grow and stretch in gradual steps. You'll soon see these practices weave a subtle and intricate tapestry of conversation inside and around you, and out to everyone with whom you connect.

Those edges you wanted to avoid will become surmountable. You may even find you welcome them because you will have practiced the techniques and built the skills to navigate them successfully — with enthusiasm, confidence and even joy.

Krista Tippet's ON BEING podcast is one of my favourite places to listen to enlightening and insightful conversations that make me think more deeply. "The purpose of speaking together differently," she says, "is to live together differently."

Conversation, I offer, is a practice that informs where life takes you. It will take you on a journey of self-insight, deeper awareness, curiosity, and exploration with others. It will open up new worlds and possibilities in front of you — because conversation is about:

- the questions you ask…
- the answers you hear…
- what you listen for…
- where you listen from…
- how you connect to others…
- caring…
- curiosity…
- unleashing possibilities in people…
- moving things forward together…
- opening up to more than you can create on your own…
- discovering answers beyond what you think possible…
- welcoming change, creativity, innovation and transformation…
- being disrupted and opened up…
- finding new edges and stepping beyond them…

My hope for you as reader is that you come to see each and every conversation as a form of sacred space in which your life and leadership are raised to a higher level.

As you practice, you'll ease away from ineffective meetings, and move toward inspiring conversations.

You'll learn more about people than you ever did before. You'll also see new possibilities in yourself and in others. You'll see people take ownership and accountability. You'll achieve more in life and in work. You'll enjoy people more, and they'll love you for it.

Conversation is so much more than social chitchat. It is fundamentally a unique part of being human, and of being in relationships with each other. That's what makes it so vital to how you lead — and how you live.

Are you ready to practice?

Your life and your leadership warrant it.

"Sing your song, friend.
Tell your story.
The map we inherited
isn't any good.
We need a new map."[2]

— SANDY CAMERON

THE PRACTICES

I've grouped the practices into five sections, mostly to give this book some structure, and to create an arc for your conversations. This is not intended as a linear or rigid framework, and you will find that many of the practices are effective in more than one stage of conversation. You might also find that some of the practices seem similar to each other. These are simply different ways for emphasising some key elements such as slowing down, listening better and asking more questions.

CONNECTING

The practices under this heading help you create real connection with others — an essential foundation for great conversation.

CARING

The practices here are designed to bring your awareness to what you truly care about and how you demonstrate your caring — for others, and to others — in the conversation.

CURIOSITY

Perhaps the most powerful area of practice, this is where you master the art and craft of asking and addressing questions that take conversations to new and insightful levels.

CLARITY

In these practices you'll notice a theme of slowing down to get really clear about how you're approaching, conducting and experiencing your conversations, and what emerges from them.

COMPLETION

These practices are the often overlooked aspects that make the difference between whether or not you leave conversations feeling you've said, done, heard and received everything you need to. Bringing your attention to completion helps you know your conversation has served you and others well, and that you can trust in what will happen as a result.

Each practice is worded as if you will practice it today. You may choose a different practice each day, yet I encourage you to focus on one practice for at least seven days at a time. Within those seven days, recommit and refocus daily on your chosen practice. Check in with yourself throughout the seven days. What are you learning? What is shifting for you as you experiment with each practice?

TABLE OF CONTENTS

CONNECTING

CONNECTING

> "Conversation is about connection in more than one sense. When two or more people connect in conversation, they often make intuitive and creative connections that spark new ideas."
>
> — JUDY APPS, *The Art of Conversation*

People want to connect with others. They want to feel connected. And they want people to connect with them.

For almost 20 years I have run an event which might be best described as a connection space for leaders. It's a week where people take time to reflect on the paths their lives have taken, and their work as leaders. And it's so much more.

It's a space where people focus on their dreams and desires, remember what they value, and connect the dots between what they've created, and how they wish to shape their future.

When we bring this group together — a myriad of strangers from different walks of life who may not appear to have much in common — the first thing we do is invite them to connect over a question that's a bit more meaningful than usual pleasantries like "How are you?" or "What do you do?"

Everyone chooses a question, and uses it to start a conversation with someone they may not have met before. The questions tend to be edgy:

- What's your deepest fear?
- What dream or ambition have you yet to fulfil?

- What inspires you to be your best?
- What message do you want to leave the next generation?

These questions stop people in their tracks. "I've never thought of that before," is a common refrain.

Within minutes, the energy in the room rises. People converse thoughtfully and animatedly. Connections have been made.

There is no fancy facilitation, or manipulation involved. Just questions that people don't normally ask, or haven't been asked before. Very quickly, strangers begin sharing deep thoughts and ideas.

I've come to a conclusion: It's very natural, and very human, to want to be in conversation at this deeper level of connection. It's what people want. It's what they enjoy. It's how they get energized. And, it's also what people are afraid of.

Perhaps it's easier to be in this level of conversation with strangers; they're not part of your everyday life. Yet, what we see time and again is that these strangers quickly become close friends. This activity forges deep connections that last way beyond a one-week event.

The practices at this first edge of conversation, CONNECTING, are designed to take you to a similar starting point. Using them will help you enter into meaningful conversation quickly, energetically and authentically.

1. CONNECT WITH THANK YOU

Ben, a C-suite executive, recently learned about a project that didn't work out the way he anticipated. One of his most trusted team members, Brian, confessed that he made a mistake, and took the blame.

Later, when Ben told me about the situation during a coaching conversation, he was proud of the fact that he didn't fly off the handle, or start criticising Brian. Instead, he asked questions.

Which is good. However, Ben's questions were actually missteps, as each one started with "Why?"

- "Why did it go wrong?"
- "Why did that happen?"
- "Why did you do that?"

Ben jumped into the problem, but didn't pay attention to how Brian felt about the situation. Nor did he acknowledge Brian's willingness to have 'fessed up to his mistakes.

Ben and Brian enjoy a good working relationship. Brian appreciates Ben's trust; he's comfortable coming to him in this type of situation.

Ben's immediate focus on the problem potentially undermined their strong connection. Brian might even doubt whether it's worth being so honest in the future.

Connecting on a personal level as the first step in conversation is key.

As I coached Ben, we walked through ways the conversation might have gone differently, and what might have happened if he'd paused to connect with Brian before jumping in.

"How might I have done that?" Ben asked me.

"What if you had simply started with a THANK YOU to Brian?"

Ben tapped himself on the forehead in a classic "doh!". He couldn't believe he missed such an obvious opportunity.

"Yes!" he reflected. "That would have led to a much better conversation."

Ben ran through a few possibilities:

"I could have slowed down and paid more attention to how Brian was feeling. He would have appreciated me acknowledging him in that way.

"I think it would have led to Brian being even more open and telling me more about what actually happened. Instead I made him defensive.

"By starting differently, our conversation would have been more creative, collaborative and productive as a whole.

"How could I have missed that? That one phrase would have made a huge difference. I'll remember next time! Thank you."

PRACTICE

Start each conversation with an authentic 'Thank You' or an acknowledgement.
Watch how the conversation progresses after this initial connection.

2. START FROM TRUST

"How do you do trust?" I ask a senior leadership team.

"Are you someone who fundamentally trusts in the goodness of others and builds relationships on the basis of that trust? Or are you someone who distrusts others and suspicously waits for them to prove whether they can be trusted?"

Your approach to trusting others influences how your conversations unfold.

When you start from distrust, you carry judgement into the conversation. Once you're stuck in judgement, it's hard to shake free. It will reflect into your language and your emotions. And you know that your state of mind will impact the other person, don't you? You might be putting them on the defensive or shutting them down.

Starting from distrust is like approaching a nearly unscalable mountain, and forcing the other person to climb it in order to have a meaningful conversation.

This lack of trust is a core piece in many organisational and societal conversations today. Without trust it's easy for things to dissolve into a pit of meaninglessness.

By contrast, when you enter into a conversation from a place of trust, you'll see, listen and learn more productively.

Paul Zak, founding director of the Center for Neuroeconomics Studies, and author of *The Trust Factor*, has studied the essential question: Why do two people trust each other in the first place? He concludes that humans are naturally inclined to trust each other, even if they don't always do so. The leadership environment they experience directly impacts the level of trust, right down to how it stimulates the 'feel-good' brain chemical oxytocin. Consider this quote from his article titled "The Neuroscience of Trust" in *Harvard Business Review:*[3]

"Employees in high-trust organizations are more productive, have more energy, collaborate better with colleagues and stay with companies longer...they also suffer less chronic stress and are happier with their lives, thus fuelling stronger performance."

In his article, Zak outlines eight ways in which leaders can enhance a culture of trust — and all eight call for different types of conversations. I recommend Zak's article if you are concerned about the levels of trust in your organisation.

When you carry a state of trust into your conversations, you engage with others in a more creative manner. There's a stark difference between this state of mind, and a brain that's stuck in the flight or fight of distrust.

It starts with the trust you place in yourself: Do you trust yourself to say what you need to say, to hear what needs to be heard, and to let others into the conversation more fully?

Conversation is the ideal space to practice trusting yourself and others.

PRACTICE

Start from trust in your meetings and conversations. Remember, trust is a conscious choice. Making this choice is an invitation to engage more meaningfully with your conversation partners.

3. BE PRESENT

Do you notice how often people, including you, might speak in the past tense?

The unconscious default to past tense creates a distance between you and your audience.

I suspect this might be a very subtle way of feeling safe, and distancing yourself from other people's reactions.

One of the simplest and most impactful ways to improve your leadership or personal presence is to firmly voice your thoughts, opinions, proposals or recommendations in the present tense:

Past Tense - Less Connection

"I was thinking we could..."
"I was recommending that..."
"I wanted to let you know..."
"Our team thought that..."

Present Tense - Stronger Connection

"I think that..."
"My recommendation is..."
"I want you to know..."
"Our team thinks..."

Try saying these aloud to yourself. How different do they sound in the present tense?

Using the present tense can upgrade your conversations, especially as a leader.

- The present tense holds you in the moment, and invites you to focus on what you are saying and hearing.
- You stay with exactly what's happening in the conversation.
- You may even grow a few inches taller as you feel the strength this very subtle language shift creates for you and those with whom you are speaking.

Many clients work with me to 'improve' what they call their executive presence. When I share this impactful tip, they immediately feel more confident, focused and grounded in what they are saying.

In short: speaking in the present tense enriches your presence.

PRACTICE

Before going into a conversation or meeting today, pause and remind yourself to speak in the present tense. This includes when you ask questions. What changes when you move from past to present?

4. LISTEN WITHOUT NOTES

Sam is a committed listener. Observing him in a coaching practice, I notice he takes a lot of notes. I suggest he listen without writing down everything he hears. He looks at me with rabbit-in-the-headlights eyes.

"I can't do that. I won't remember anything. I don't want to miss anything important. I always take notes."

Do you rely on taking notes?

- Taking notes can be a way of staying in control of the conversation.
- You may take notes in case you 'get it wrong' and need to later prove what was said.

Consider this: what do you miss each time you drop your head to write down a note?

You might miss someone's expression, their emotion, their discomfort, their confusion or their joy. You might not notice when they are thinking more deeply about your question or comment.

Is it possible you can't trust your memory to recall what you hear because you don't listen well enough in the first place? What if the piece of information you are missing never made its way to your brain, because you were busy taking notes?

When you split your attention between listening and taking notes, you're unable to fully take things in.

On this occasion, Sam eventually agrees to try listening without his pen in hand. At the end of the conversation, he is smiling. He is relaxed. He pats his conversation partner on the shoulder.

"How was it?" I ask. "Did you miss your pen?"

He laughs.

"At first I did. It was strange not to have something to do with my hands. Then I found I listened more deeply."

Sam continues.

"I watched my partner's eyes more. And because I didn't have any notes, I discovered that the conversation flowed from what she was saying, not from what I'd written down. It was magical. It was more fun. I felt more engaged. And my partner seemed freer to talk when she didn't think I was taking notes. I'm going to do this more often."

PRACTICE

Experiment with not taking notes while listening to another person, or during a meeting. Notice how your focus changes. Take a few moments after the conversation ends to record important details, reminders and actions.

5. DON'T INTERRUPT

"I realised I was only listening till the other person stopped talking, so that I could talk."

You have a brilliant, quick and sharp-witted mind that thinks faster than the other person is talking. In fact, your mind is already making up ITS MIND what it wants to say next — and it can't wait.

Interrupting is common.

Take time to listen at the office and at home this week for how often someone around you starts talking before someone else has finished.

The interrupter is eager to get his or her thoughts into the conversation. However, interrupting may lead to unwittingly disregarding the importance of what the other person is saying.

My colleague, Phil, is a world-class listener. He has a simple rule: he counts quietly to eight before he starts to speak after someone else has been talking.

When you're in conversation with Phil, there's a lot happening in that pause before he speaks:

- There's the time it takes for you to say something.
- There's the time it takes for what you've said to reach Phil's brain so he can truly hear it.
- Then, there's the time it takes for his brain to process what you've said.
- From there, it takes more time for Phil's brain to decide what he wants to say in response.
- Finally, it takes time for Phil to form and translate his thoughts into words that come out of his mouth.

The entire sequence happens in the blink of an eye. And then it repeats itself in your brain as you consider your response to what Phil says.

As the world keeps speeding up, you may feel ever-increasing pressure to get your words in edgewise. There might be little or no space for full listening, or for thoughtful consideration of what you want to say.

Slowing down can lead to a richer conversation.

All it takes is silently counting to eight, and enjoying the pause. And, in my experience, there's often a beautiful moment of eye contact and personal connection in those eight seconds of wondering what the other person is about to say next.

PRACTICE

Count how many times you manage NOT to interrupt someone when they are speaking today. You might even check before you speak with a polite question such as, "Do you have anything else to say on that?"

6. SEE THE PERSON BEHIND THE LABEL

It is the first morning of our week-long leadership intensive in the Canadian Rockies. This group met for the first time 12 hours earlier. As people connect over questions, I hear exclamations of surprise. I see smiles and twinkles in their eyes.

They are learning about the real people beyond the job titles that label them.

They quickly decide that there will be no labels as they learn together this week. Instead, each will speak human-to-human, seeking to see one another as a real person, without getting caught up in judgements or assumptions.

Even when people have worked together for years, there is always something new to learn about each other.

When you listen beyond labels and job titles, you'll hear people say things like:

"It's so much more fun."
"It's more genuine."
"Everyone is interested."
"I never knew that about you before."
"We're a lot alike."

A client recently told me he couldn't say what he really wanted to say to his boss about a frustrating situation. Yet the only real way forward for his conversation was to stop labelling his boss as 'the boss,' and to speak with him as a real person.

It's a two-way street. Dropping labels can help you see that there's a real person who's quite possibly more like you than you think.

We might share job titles, but we're each unique. Therefore, we deserve to be seen and heard in our own right.

PRACTICE

Use each person's name during conversations and meetings today. Aim to not generalise about people by labelling them with their job title or function.

7. GET OUT AND TALK WITH PEOPLE

I confess I had relegated Tom Peters and his management thinking to the archives of my brain. Surely, there must be newer ideas around some 30 years later?

However, when I hear him on a recent podcast,[4] I discover that he's still talking about leading by walking about — just as he did in his seminal book, *In Search of Excellence*.

Tom Peters' ideas hold good today — perhaps even more so. You see, it's not just about the walking. It's about the talking, and the connections and conversations you have while you walk about.

That's where the treasure lies.

Gone are the days of being shut in the corner office.

- As one of today's leaders, you are out and about, showing your face and talking with people.
- You ask questions to find out what's on people's mind, and to discover what they need from you.
- You discover where people are challenged, worried or stressed.
- You uncover where they are inspired, learning and excelling.

Walking doesn't always mean actually walking. These days, it may take the shape of virtual visits using conference call lines and video forums, to cross the physical divide and talk with colleagues, friends and even your family around the globe.

In the podcast, Peters relates a now-classic story of a senior executive who starts her day with a half-hour walkabout, no matter how piled up her desk is with papers. Not only does she invariably learn something new from her walkabout conversations, but somehow, when she comes back to her office, her pile of paperwork seems lighter and less worrisome.

She's energised and enlightened by seeing the world through the eyes of others. And the best part is that her conversations are never one-sided.

- What will people give you in return when you go out and have conversations with them?
- What help might you ask for and receive?

This isn't just about the workplace. It also applies to parents, siblings, cousins, great aunts or long lost friends you haven't spoken with in a while.

What conversation is waiting on your next walkabout?

PRACTICE

Get out and talk with people. Ask questions. Listen to what's going on in their world. Who haven't you talked with in a while? Who are you avoiding?

8. SPEAK UP WITH A QUESTION

Douglas is very good at his highly technical job. Yet he's so quiet, he rarely, if ever, speaks up or brings his ideas to the table.

Douglas admits to me, in a coaching conversation, that he doesn't feel he should challenge his team leader's ideas. He's afraid that if he does, it will seem like he's challenging or criticising the team leader, which could get him fired. Instead, he defers to his leader's ideas, even when he knows there are better solutions.

I suggest that Douglas start with a question when he wants to speak up with his ideas.

Starting with a question is a great way to open what might feel like a difficult conversation — even when it's with someone you perceive as an authority.

It works well for Douglas.

- Using questions helps him feel curious and creative, and less combative.
- In addition, he can use his ideas and solutions in his questions.
- This way, he feels like he's offering ideas, not trying to justify them to others.
- Finally, he realises people are listening more to what he says.

Douglas' hesitation about speaking up soon disappears. In the process, he also makes another big discovery: He had more to lose by not speaking up. By remaining quiet, his leader could have easily drawn the conclusion that Douglas had nothing to share. He might never have known how many smart solutions Douglas could offer.

He might have even decided to hire a more talkative person to fill Douglas' post. Thankfully, Douglas now speaks up, so it never came to that.

Opening conversations with questions became Douglas' lifeline.

When I see him a few weeks later, Douglas is almost jumping around with excitement at how busy and involved he is. He's learned:

- His team leader does want him to speak up with his ideas.
- His questions help his team leader think things through.
- His leader genuinely doesn't have all the answers.
- He's found the confidence to share his expertise.

Starting a conversation with a question helps to get your creative juices flowing, and may get your ideas, possibilities and solutions heard and acted upon.

PRACTICE

Put your ideas forward in the form of a question. Starting with "What if...?" often works.
Do you find it easier to get your ideas across now that you're using questions?

9. ANSWER THE QUESTION THAT'S ASKED

Listen carefully in your next meeting or conversation. Are you or those around you answering the question that's actually asked? Or, are you answering the question you think you heard?

This can make for a confusing conversation!

It can end up a bit like like the classic "four candles/fork handles" bit on *The Two Ronnies*, a British sketch comedy show.[5]

Sometimes, the conversations in my household are as equally comedic:

"Would you like tea or coffee?"
"I'm just going to the shop."
"That doesn't answer my question."
"I'll be back in half an hour."

I wind up making tea anyway, and it's obvious that we're in two different conversations at once.

How can you make sure you answer the question someone is actually asking?

Here's a simple technique: repeat the question back before answering it! This will:

- Confirm that you've heard the question correctly, and are respectful of the person who asks it.
- Let your brain hear the question again so you can tune in more specifically.
- Give you time to formulate a thoughtful answer, rather than blurting out an answer that might come from the thoughts in your head instead of what the other person has actually asked.

Checking that you've heard the question that's actually been asked is also another way to test your listening skills.

PRACTICE

Listen attentively when someone asks you a question, and repeat it back to ensure you answer exactly what's been asked. "So, what you're asking me is…"

CARING

CARING

"Some people talk to you in their free time.
Some people free their time to talk with you."

— ANONYMOUS

"Kind is the new cool."

I spot this slogan on a young girl's T-shirt as she passes by me in the street. I love it. Imagine how the world could be a better place if everyone wore, and believed in this slogan.

You don't have to rush out and buy the T-shirt though. Instead, you can bring CARING into your conversations.

I bet you can recall a time when you or someone else stomped petulantly away from a conversation, mumbling something along the lines of, "Do what you want. I don't care anyway."

Don't turn away. Instead, take on the practices in this second edge of the conversation. They invite you to start showing that you do care.

- You care about what's important to you.
- You care that you show up in a manner that will be productive and useful.
- And, you care that others do the same.

On a recent edition of Sam Harris' *Making Sense* podcast, Johann Hari referenced an American study that showed how only a few years ago, people had, on average, five other people they could talk with when they needed a listening ear.[6] Today, he suggests that many of these same people would say they have no one who cares enough to be there for them. Siri, Alexa and text messaging just don't cut it.

Let's bring caring back, starting with caring to have real conversations with each other.

The conversation space is a not-to-be-missed opportunity to show someone you care about their life, work, challenges, successes, and about them as a person. You care about what they find important, their ideas, and their opinions.

Over the years, I've seen companies spend millions on anonymous engagement and feedback surveys. Working with an inspiring group of leaders recently, the first thing they said when they received anonymous survey results — where people shared feedback on them as leaders — was, "I wish this wasn't anonymous. I'd love to have real conversations with the people who gave this feedback. I really care to know them, and to discuss it further so I can learn from it."

Caring invites you to be open and ready to be surprised by the deep sentiment and trust that emerges in return.

If you can be more caring in your daily conversations, you might even save time and money by NOT conducting anonymous surveys.

Instead, you'll be having real conversations, and directly hearing what everyone cares about.

When people care about something, it energises, engages and moves them to action. In fact, it may ultimately be the one thing that does.

10. GO SLOW TO GO FAST

Like many clients, Abby starts off our coaching conversation by declaring she's overwhelmed. There are just not enough hours in her day to successfully navigate the competing demands of a challenging leadership role, the life of a soccer mum to teenage sons, and having a husband who must travel for work five days a week. Add to that the fact that her father is in the hospital with a suspected heart attack, and you can appreciate the speed at which Abby's life is unfolding.

"Unravelling out of control," is what it feels like to her.

An hour later, Abby has caught her breath.

- She's visibly more relaxed as we talk through a tough decision she needs to make about one of her team members at work.
- On the personal front, she draws up a rota to make sure family members get to their respective events.
- And, she's identified a window of time that she can spend with her father in the hospital.

Sometimes it's just about slowing down.

In a world that seems to be constantly speeding up, slowing down to get to the life you truly want is quite possibly the most common piece of work I do with clients. And it takes practice.

- It's the only way you can find your way out of overwhelm to a place of controlled calm and focus.
- It's the only way you can search inside yourself for what's most important to you.

And, it's one way to challenge yourself and your team by asking deeper questions that lead to innovative and creative ways forward.

I just heard from another client about a challenge her team took on to solve a business problem. The quick-fix would have been to hire consultants, then settle on a pre-fabbed solution that didn't fit.

Instead, she slowed her team down, and gave them time to come up with their own solution. As it turns out, their new solution is a completely revolutionary product that no consultant or organisation had come up with. It quite possibly could put her team on the map as industry-leading innovators.

That's what I call going slow to go fast.

In his book, *A More Beautiful Question*, Warren Berger, a New York journalist, describes a process of question-storming. He encourages teams to slow down long enough to ask as many as 45 questions, in order to arrive at a true difference-making breakthrough.

You might agree that not many of your meetings would stay with a question that long without feeling like things were too slow. Yet this slowness might just be what makes the difference.

PRACTICE

Slow down enough to fully express what you want to say.
Listen deeply to ensure you've heard and understood what others are saying.
Create more time for yourself and others to think.

11. THE GIFT OF SILENCE

It is the last morning of a three-day coaching skills course I'm running for middle managers at a large drinks company in the UK. John is struggling to keep quiet while his conversation partner speaks.

"If I'm not adding something to the conversation," he says to me, "then I don't feel like I'm giving the other person anything. They expect to get something from me. After all, I'm their leader. I need to be giving them something, don't I?"

"What happens when you don't speak, John?" I ask.

He thinks for a moment.

"I guess the other person gets time to think, and to put her ideas forward," he says.

"Isn't that what you want to happen?"

I used the quote from the movie, *Powder*, in my last book, *Asking Great Questions*. I love it so much, it's worth repeating here in the context of silence. It goes like this:

"Have you ever listened to people from the inside? Listened so close you can hear their thoughts and all their memories, hear them think from the places they don't even know they think from?"

Do you define your value by how much you speak, or by how often you listen?

Do you feel you have little value if you're not adding in your ideas, opinions, answers or experience? In doing so, might you inadvertently squeeze out the other person's thoughts, ideas, opinions and needs?

One of the greatest gifts we can give to each other is the opportunity to be heard.

As the well-known adage goes, we have one mouth and two ears, so let's use them in that proportion.

In his YouTube video, "Learn to Listen," Simon Sinek takes this one step further.[7] He suggests that as a manager, you ought to practice being the last to speak, in order to really hear what others are thinking, and where their ideas come from. When you speak first, you have already set the tone and direction of the conversation.

When you listen for what you don't know, and when you wait to share your opinions until after hearing from others, you will come to see, as my middle manager client did, that the silence you create becomes a GIFT for everyone — one that keeps on giving.

PRACTICE

Start each meeting or conversation with a moment of silence.
Ask what other people think. As you invite their ideas, be willing to speak last.
Enjoy giving the gift of silence, and of discovering what appears in the space it creates.

12. STAY OUT OF THE STORY

The one conversation tip that shifted everything for me as a coach and leader was when I learned the distinction between process and the content of the story.

Up till that point, my contribution to any conversation had been to get caught up in the story being discussed. I didn't see how I could play a different role in the conversation.

As a coach, my job today is to avoid getting embroiled in the client's story.

To do so, I ask questions that inspire clients to shift their story, to look at things from a new perspective, and to find ideas and solutions that move their story forward.

I don't need to add in my opinions, or offer answers. In fact, I learn the most by staying out of the story. When I sit back, my thinking, attention and awareness work in new ways. Instead of being part of their story, I become an observer and listener. As our conversation unfolds, I'm invited to ask questions, and listen at new levels.

You can see this for yourself in conversations too. Take the classic example of when someone has been somewhere exotic on holiday, and they want to tell you about it. As you listen, consider:

- Is your mind already drifting to your own holidays, and comparing stories (content)? Or, are you listening so intently that you don't even think of your own holiday experiences?

- Are you genuinely curious to hear more about their experience?
- Do you ask questions to understand why they chose a specific holiday, what it meant to them, how they felt to be away, what it meant for them to create such a memory, or even how they returned enriched, or in a better state of mind?

These types of process questions ultimately create a stronger connection, letting the storyteller feel truly heard and appreciated.

Asking them does two important things:

- You help the storyteller relive their holiday experience.
- You encourage them to ask you about your holiday experiences. When they do, it's their turn to listen.

Imagine a similar conversation in your workplace.

As a leader, if you converse at the content level, you end up putting in your thoughts and ideas, and not fully appreciating the other person's experience.

When you stay in process — i.e. out of the story, like a facilitator or a coach — you fulfil your prime responsibility, which is to inspire people to grow, stretch, learn and discover more about themselves and their capabilities.

PRACTICE

Get clear on your role. Can you see when you are caught up in the story? Do you need to be IN the story? Or, do you need to help the other person move their story toward possibilities and actions?

13. BE MINDFUL OF YOUR INTENTION

Years ago, I managed an innovative high-street learning centre. My intention was to build a culture of ownership, empowerment and trust. Team members were used to hearing questions from me that inspired them to learn, grow and provide great service. I experimented with giving them as much scope to use their initiative as I could.

One day, I found myself in a rather harassed state of mind. I don't remember why I felt so stressed that day, but its consequences stick with me like it happened yesterday.

Momentarily forgetting my true intention as a leader, I walked through the store and noticed team members bantering with each other. As I walked past them, I heard a rather abrupt question come out of my mouth: "Don't you have some work to be getting on with?"

I broke so many of my own rules in that moment: I didn't take time to find out what was really going on; I didn't think through my words and their impact; and I didn't stop to look at the situation through the eyes of my employees.

I simply threw out an offhand question that felt cold and mean. My inner monster had taken over.

Instantly I felt bad, but my monster's grip was fierce that day. I carried on to my office and closed the door.

Moments later, a team member named William came to check if I was okay. After all, he said, this was out of character for me, and the entire team were concerned.

Thankfully, our culture of trust and openness was working. And it was coming back to me. I apologised immediately.

I closed the door after William left and took some reflection time. I realised I had not been mindful of my higher intention as a leader, or how my comment would be received.

Had I been, I would have shifted my focus to curiosity and caring for my team's situation. Were they bored? Did they need something? Were they exploring new ideas to improve our service?

Bringing myself back to mindful awareness, rather than reactions and assumptions, shook me out of my funk. I remembered that being intentional is far more essential than succumbing to the heat of the moment.

Even as leaders, sometimes we need help to stay mindfully aware around how we show up in every conversation. Every thought, comment, question, behaviour and expression can be interpreted differently by those on the receiving end.

Gone are the days when parents or teachers repeatedly demanded we pay attention. Nowadays, we must hold ourselves to that attention, and be mindful of our interactions at all times.

Your intention will influence the way you word a question, the tone you use, and the impact your question leaves behind. Pay attention. Are you feeling rushed? Are you bristly? What will others truly hear when you speak?

PRACTICE

Before you ask anyone anything, ask yourself: "What is my intention here?"
Be mindful of your words and tone.

14. INSPIRATION, NOT INTERFERENCE

Cathy spends several hours of her busy schedule sourcing a venue for an important client event. She is confident she has negotiated a good value deal at a venue that will impress clients.

It hits her pretty hard when she presents her recommendation to her manager, who suggests that Cathy contact a friend of his who owns another venue.

Disheartened but compliant, Cathy makes one more call, and asks for a quote. Yes, her manager's friend will host their event, and they can save an almost negligible amount of money too.

Nominal cost savings aside, something gets lost in this process.

Cathy had wanted to take responsibility for the decision. In fact, she thought she had been given ownership of the process. She felt inspired to make a good choice that balanced the needs of the event, with a responsible financial decision.

Then her manager interfered. At least, that's what it felt like to Cathy:

- The additional savings didn't justify the time Cathy had already invested in the project.
- The outcome left Cathy feeling dejected, as if her time and decision-making process were essentially worthless in the eyes of her manager. It's impossible to put a price on that.

If her manager was always going to take back these types of decisions, thinking he had a better solution, then what was the point in having Cathy put in the effort in the first place?

If he was going to eliminate the inspiration she felt this time, what would stop him from interfering again? How would Cathy ever feel like she could fully own a project without the fear of such interference?

Imagine how inspired Cathy might have been to know that her hard work had paid off, and that in the eyes of her manager, her choice and proposal of venue served the objective well.

Inspiration — instead of interference, where you inadvertently give ownership with one hand and take it back with another — is priceless.

PRACTICE

Take time to look at things through the other person's eyes. Imagine their experience. What inspires and empowers them to take ownership of decisions you want them to lead?

15. MAKE EVERYONE RIGHT, NOT WRONG

I love this long quote from Ken Wilber:

"I have one major rule: everybody is right. More specifically, everybody — including me — has some important pieces of truth, and all of those pieces need to be honoured, cherished, and included in a more gracious, spacious, and compassionate embrace."[8]

No one sets out to be intentionally wrong. It can seem like people make each other wrong when they are simply asserting different views and perspectives. Everyone is trying to establish their own worth and value, and in most cases do not mean to flex their 'I'll show you I'm right' muscles.

What if you don't have to use up your energy proving you're right, and, in doing so, making others wrong? What if you used that energy instead to listen more deeply.

As the Wilber quote illustrates, many voices combine to bring a richer perspective to every situation.

As a leader, parent, big sister, older brother, friend or colleague, you will gain more when you approach conversations with the desire and compassion to hear everyone's piece of the truth.

And here's a very simple, almost imperceptible, conversation tip to help you do this: drop the 'but'.

You don't realise you're doing it. Yet imagine one of your team members has put blood, sweat and tears into a presentation. She's proud of what she's done. Her presentation gets a great reception from others. You walk up to her afterwards and say something along the lines of, "Great presentation… BUT do you think you could have…"

You just burst her bubble and negated all the good feeling she had about her work. She's likely wondering why she bothered to work so hard, especially when that little word negates everything she's done right, and makes it sound like you're only focusing on what's wrong.

Is that how you want people to experience you as a leader: like you always focus on what's wrong?

My colleague (and accountability partner for getting this book done) Betty Healey is known as the Roadsigns Coach. "Dropping that three-letter word, and not making others wrong, is a powerful technique in teams," she says. "It shifts relationships from arguments and competition, to conversation, connection and collaboration."

If you keep 'butting' people, why would they bother to put their ideas forward at all? What if their piece of the truth never comes to the fore?

When you consciously eliminate one small, three-letter word, it creates a world more 'right' for everyone.

PRACTICE
Read the Ken Wilber quote daily. Consciously replace your 'but' with 'thank you' to appreciate and consider everyone's piece of the truth.

16. THE BEAUTY OF EMPATHY

You may have heard the oft-quoted phrase, "Be interested rather than interesting."[9] Sounds good, but what does it mean to put it into practice?

In my work, I get to show up as a caring listener and say very little. I'm much more interested in my clients than they are in me. It truly is ALL about them.

I think this is one reason why people choose to have conversations with independent, neutral coaches, rather than with members of their teams, or even their family.

For years, I thought empathy meant appreciating another person's experience or point of view, without being involved in it, and that responding with phrases like "I know how you feel," showed empathy.

Real empathy is more than that. You might even say it's the opposite to that.

Rowan Williams, former Archbishop of Canterbury, suggests that true empathy is "entering into a conversation with the awareness that I can't possibly know how you feel."

After all, your experience is unique to you. Mine is unique to me. No matter how similar we consider our experiences to be, all we can do is listen deeply, and give each other space to be heard.

If this book were to achieve only one thing, I want it to inspire a greater sense of empathy — especially in the world of business and politics.

We can move toward solutions quicker when we appreciate and learn from the ways that others experience the world. And, if we can truly hear these differences, then we can find the threads that connect them to ours. Together, we can channel our energy creatively toward finding ways forward.

We'd spend less time arguing and defending our views. We'd even skip the part where we try to score points over each other.

This is an area of real concern for future generations. Sherry Turkle, in her book, *Reclaiming Conversation,* has researched the impact of today's mobile phone and social media culture. She highlights the fact that today's young people are growing up without developing the capacity for empathy.

Our technology helps us avoid real, caring conversations. We can use our tools to shield us from making emotional connections. Turkle cites a family that even argues by text, because things are "too emotional to speak about" in person.

That's a far cry from stepping into conversations, and showing real empathy for each other.

PRACTICE

Enter conversations with an awareness of caring for the other person. Start from this assumption: You can have no real understanding of their experience. Listen deeply.

17. CHECK YOUR DEFAULT

I'm coaching with Joe, an executive client who is going on holiday. I ask who will hold the fort and have authority to make key decisions in his absence?

As professionals, it's easy to assume default positions pretty quickly.

In this case, Joe says he'll pass the authority up the tree to the experienced leaders above him. This is a clear default solution.

I gently stop him mid-sentence. I'm concerned he's going for the quick and easy 'fix' and not considering other possibilities.

As a leader, Joe prides himself on giving others the chance to grow and learn. His absence on holiday is precisely such an opportunity.

"What if somoeone on your team takes over while you're away?" I ask.

Joe's default could have helped him make an easy and logical short-term choice. By pressing beyond his edge, Joe saw greater possibilities for his team — and for his own leadership.

As the saying goes, "If you only do what you've always done, you only get what you always got. And you'll always get what you've always got, if you only think as you've always thought."[10]

Catching default moments, and being willing to stretch beyond your edge, can bring you closer to what you really care about in a leadership situation.

Venturing beyond your edge might be key.

But how can you safely venture beyond your edge?

Here are three essential questions to ask yourself:

- Is this how I always look at situations like these?
- What might I be missing?
- How can I look at this differently?

PRACTICE

Before you finalise any decision or action, pause. Then ask yourself the three essential questions above. If your answers point somewhere new, go there.

18. DON'T ASSUME

Here are two short anecdotes from my brief history of making horrible assumptions:

- My niece refers me to the owner of a company that she's recently discovered. She thinks I can help them out. Something about the person's name comes across as a little unusual (to me at least), and when I make my initial phone call, I expect to hear a male voice on the other end of the line. And, of course…it's a woman.
- I meet a female executive leader for the first time at a conference. She and I chat over coffee during a break. She begins telling me how she's lived in several countries. "Was it your husband's job that took you to so many places?" I ask, without thinking. As soon as those words are out my mouth I know I've put my foot in it. "Oh no," she says, "it was my job with a global corporation that took our family around the world." I was embarrassed, and had no way to take back my question with even the slightest bit of grace. She ignored me for the rest of the weekend. I couldn't blame her. I was such an idiot in that moment.

It's easy to make assumptions. They're buried deep in our unconscious, and take over when we least expect them to.

How can we keep from letting our assumptions hold us captive? Here are some key practices from this book that might help:

- Listen. Listen. Listen. You can't do enough listening.
- Pause and consider what you want to say before saying it.
- Start with a question.
- Slow your mind down and focus on the other person.

Had I simply asked an open question such as, "What took you overseas?" she would have had the opportunity to enlighten me. And I would have had the chance to listen and learn more about her motivations — and about her adventures.

Who knows how our relationship might have evolved differently? We might have come together, rather than drifted apart.

If only I'd heard my own assumption!

PRACTICE

Listen for your assumptions before you speak. When you're about to make an assumption, either call it out ("I'm making an assumption here") or set it aside. Ask the other person a genuinely curious question. Curiosity will trump assumptions every time.

19. START WITH APPRECIATION

"I appreciate you and our conversations. They make a big difference for me at the moment."

This comes from Betty, a friend who's recently undergone two knee surgeries. She's feeling a little shut off from the professional world right now — a world in which she is usually active.

Our conversations mean a lot to her. They remind her of the experienced coach and consultant she yearns to return to being when she is mobile again.

When I hear her heartfelt words, they land deep in my heart. I receive many 'thank you' messages from day to day. However, no one but Betty expressly says they appreciate me.

Her words make me feel seen and heard.

We've all been taught that saying 'thank you' is good manners. Yet in our busy world, the phrase often comes across as little more than a polite throwaway as people are leaving a meeting room — if it's said at all.

On the other hand, appreciation is a powerful motivator...and much more.

The Appreciative Inquiry movement[11] has proven that acknowledging the 'root causes of success' is an underutilised methodology for building successful relationships, teams, businesses and societies. It works on the assumption that if we can identify specifically the positive drivers that lead to the results we seek, then we can build on them to create even more success.

Consider the dual meaning of the word appreciate. On one hand, when we appreciate something or someone, we acknowledge them in a meaningful way. Then there's the other appreciate — as in a treasure, antique or piece of art that gains value over time.

When Betty says she appreciates me, it helps me see the increased value in our conversations.

Appreciating those around you, the efforts they contribute, and the successful results they help you achieve will increase value for everyone.

I like to share this concept with clients who refer to themselves as problem solvers. I always say, "If you're constantly looking for problems, then that's what you'll find. And, you'll create more problems in order to solve them."

Then I follow that up with a very direct question: "When did you last express full appreciation for what your team has achieved?"

Often, it's met with silence.

PRACTICE

Where do you show appreciation? Among friends? Family? What about in the workplace?
Choose someone to whom you might say "I appreciate you."
Track how this changes your experience with them.

20. THE L WORD

In 1997, when we started IC International in Scotland, we came across a book called *Reclaiming Higher Ground* by Lance Secretan, a Canadian leadership guru. We loved Secretan's concepts for creating organisations that truly inspire the heart and soul of people.

Here's one of the questions he asks people to answer when it's time to assess the soul of an organisation:

"Do I love what I do and who I do it with?"

LOVE was not a word I had encountered in my corporate career up to that point. It wasn't long before we started to test it out within our own team.

Could we say we love each other? The question led to endless hours of conversation to explore the many different kinds of love in the world. Finally, we compromised with a coded email signature when writing to each other: we'd sign off "OTAL," which meant "love, On The Appropriate Layer."

Initially, we didn't dare end any client emails with the word 'love' anywhere near the signature line. Strangely (or maybe not), the more we used the word 'love' in little experimental ways, the more we came to realise that love IS love: a powerful force in conversations and in relationships of any kind.

Gradually, we came to use 'love' in our correspondence and conversations with clients. I can still remember the day I heard it used within a client workshop.

It touched me to the core when my client group spoke of how much they loved their work, and the people they worked with. And they truly meant it.

"What made you cry when we spoke today, Aileen?" they asked over dinner that evening. I was able to tell them it had to do with how long I'd waited to hear the word 'love' used so genuinely and authentically in a work setting.

Another early client, a senior executive in a large oil corporation, always came from love. She'd say things like, "Aileen, I need you to pull your socks up and get this completed by Friday — and I love you for what you bring to the team."

Immediately I'd feel more energised and committed to pulling my socks up for her.

The power of love always inspired me more than any tough words, or gung-ho motivation. And that's still the case.

It was with joy that I recently read an interview with Kevin Plank, on the culture of his company, Under Armour. "We're winning," he says. "(People) are feeling loved and cared for and they're loving and caring for each other."[12] A winning culture indeed.

At last we're reaching a new edge. It is becoming acceptable to work from, with and through love. And one of the easiest ways to bring love into the workplace is through conversation.

PRACTICE

Use the word LOVE as much as you can, even if it feels uncomfortable at the start. If you want people to love what they do, saying the word 'love' will help complete the circle.

CURIOSITY

CURIOSITY

"We keep moving forward, opening new doors, and doing new things, because we're curious, and curiosity keeps leading us down new paths."

— WALT DISNEY

I have a tendency to accept things at face value. I was never trained to question things more deeply, or to be really curious. Until, that is, I learned that the most amazing conversations happen when I forget everything I think I know, and get really curious to learn, understand and hear more.

By now, I've actually become known for asking questions that don't otherwise get asked.

You'll have heard time and again how many of us are programmed from our school days to stop at the 'right' answer.

I didn't get applauded for questioning the prevailing point of view...for being curious enough to explore beyond what's already known...or to go to the edge of my current understanding and assumptions in order to uncover new perspectives and insights. Did you?

I never learned to effectively enter what I now like to call the 'I don't know' space.

One of the best leaders I ever met liked to say that his strengths were in stepping into his 'don't know' space. Whenever he didn't know something, he would stay curious and ask more questions in order to gain a deeper understanding and level of knowing.

Conversations with him were great. We'd spend hours exploring and expanding on ideas in a state of mutual curiosity.

I'll often hear people say they have an open mind. They rarely mean it, and often respond automatically from what they already know.

Citing Warren Berger again, his *Book of Beautiful Questions* stretches the concept of opening your mind with this challenging question:

"Are you willing to open up your mind to the possibility that what you think you know is limiting you?"

Far from killing cats, true curiosity takes you into wide open spaces where you:

- Hear what you're not yet hearing.
- See what you've been overlooking.
- Learn the missing pieces.
- Fill the gaps in your awareness.

Curiosity is literally the means by which you can expand conversations into new areas of discovery, satisfaction and collective growth. It can be quite powerful when you let your unknowing lead the way.

21. LISTENING FOR VS. LISTENING FROM

"They're stopping our bus service!" My mother's voice is angry and impatient on the other end of the phone. "It's going to play havoc with my routine. I won't be able to get to all my activities."

This sudden change comes as a bolt out of the blue to an active, independent, elderly lady who relies on the local bus service as a lifeline.

A week later, we are at a public meeting with the council officers who have made the decision to change the service. Like many bureaucratic systems, it becomes a good example of listening FROM their own perspective, rather than listening FOR what serves the needs of their users.

It had seemed totally okay to the council officers to change the bus service, based on what they heard in their worldview:

"Bus services are no longer viable. We've got some budget funding to spend. We need to be more eco-friendly. We can't afford to run empty buses…" And so on. In their minds, an on-demand service in place of the current time-tabled service would be more efficient.

It all makes sense to them. Sadly, they're not listening FOR what people need. They haven't asked any questions of the users.

Without curiosity about their riders' needs, the council misses the point: the bus means so much to this little community. It is a lifeline to get to appointments, a social channel for meeting people, and an escape from isolation and loneliness. It's even an avenue to adventure that connects riders with bus services to other towns and cities. Some people catch a bus to see where it takes them, and end up enjoying a bowl of soup at a picturesque beach-side cafe.

Being able to walk out the door and catch a bus is a symbol of independence. Keeping this independence is what matters most.

The major flaw was that the council members had not spoken with riders before they made their decision to change the bus service. No one asked riders what they needed, or bothered listening to how they live.

Sadly, this kind of decision is all-too-often replicated in many organisations. The powers that be make decisions because they are listening FROM their view of the world. They're not listening FOR what others need.

If you're only listening FROM your own perspective, you're missing a great deal of information — and missing out on knowing how certain changes will affect your people.

PRACTICE

Practice 360° listening today.
What changes when you listen FOR another person's perspective and understanding?
Does it help you discover what's needed to resolve a situation?

22. LISTENING IN LAYERS

I'm standing on one of the most beautiful beaches on the western coast of Vancouver Island. It's a windy day. I listen.

First, I hear the roar of the surf as it rears up to take its wave-like form a few hundred meters out at sea.

I watch as it undulates, gathers force, then suddenly crashes over itself in a cascade of foaming power.

Then it quiets down and breaks gently against my toes, rushing sand all around me.

If I listen very carefully, there's an almost imperceptible sucking sound as the water ebbs back over the sand, retreating from the shore to be part of the next roller.

In the stillness between waves, I become aware of more sounds. The wind whips through the trees farther up the bank behind me. Gulls screech as they swoop and swirl overhead. In the distance, a child cries and calls for her mother.

Then I hear the echoes of the waves once more, and my inner voice tells me it's time to move. As soon as I do, my focus shifts to what's next.

It's getting dark. How long will it take me to get home? Do I need to pick anything up for supper? Did I remember to shut off the iron before I left earlier?

Then my phone rings. I often don't answer in the midst of such a powerful moment in nature, but I recognise the number and swipe to take the call. Now, I'm listening to my sister's voice.

"Do you know where Mother is?"

She sounds tired and excited at the same time. I hear my own exhaustion, and pretend it's nothing as I cheerily reply.

Layers and layers of listening, with so much to be heard.

As humans, we yearn to be heard. It's a practice of depth and love. My friend and colleague, Gary Diggins, calls us to "listen each other into wholeness" through the many layers waiting to be explored, inquired into and heard more deeply.

Here's a practice I like to do to test my own listening: I'll tune in to my favourite podcast, news show, or radio program. (Podcasts are best for this, since I can go back and re-listen later.) I'll listen for one minute, then I'll cut the volume and write down what I heard. Then, I go back and re-listen to see how accurate I was. Over time, I'll build this practice up to longer durations, going for two, three, or maybe even five minutes. It's an interesting and powerful way to test my listening.

Leaving the beach, I greet my husband when I get home.

"How was your day?" he asks.

"Fine," I say blithely, resorting to the superficial layer that passes for everyday listening, yet leaves me unfulfilled and disconnected.

So many layers below remain untouched and unheard.

PRACTICE

Find a quiet moment, no matter where you are.
Bring your attention to the layers of sound around and inside you.
What do you hear that you haven't heard before?

23. ASK THE SCARY QUESTIONS

In my coaching work, I've found that the question that feels scary or uncomfortable is often the exact question that leads to a new insight or a breakthrough in someone's thinking.

It's a real edge when you hear a question in your head that wants to be asked — and that you want to ask — but you're afraid of what will happen if you ask it.

What holds you back from asking that scary question? Perhaps it's one of the following:

- Fear of looking silly, upsetting someone or getting upset.
- Fear that the conversation will get emotionally charged.
- Fear of hearing an answer you don't want to hear, and the consequences that might follow.

'Scary' doesn't mean asking an aggressive, threatening or bullying question. Instead, it means you don't know whether it's okay to ask the question, or that you're afraid to ask it.

Not asking the scary question is a symptom of something I call polite mediocrity. It leads to unasked questions, incomplete conversations, unsatisfying results and empty living.

Let's go back to the word 'scary' for a moment. Maybe we need to change the label. After all, if you believe something is scary, the belief might hold you back from taking an important step.

What if you think of them as 'bold' or 'edgy' questions instead? Like on *Star Trek*, they'll "boldly go where no one has gone before." Wouldn't that be an exciting mindset to adopt and rely on when it comes to asking questions?

Whether you call them scary, edgy, bold or something else, the secret to asking such questions is to be totally open to whatever answer comes back.

The fear that comes up when you think of the question might not be about the question at all. It might be about the answer you assume or imagine you'll receive.

When you get stuck in your own narrative of what might happen, you're not really open to what is happening, or what will happen. To truly know, you have to step over the edge and ask the question that wants to be asked.

Can you?

PRACTICE

To boldly go! Take a deep breath, then ask the question you don't want to ask. You don't know what will happen until you do.

24. OPEN YOUR QUESTIONS

Chloe is a very successful sales person. She loves her clients and goes the extra mile to help them find solutions for their business. Her challenge comes at the final step of securing a full commitment from some clients. They tend to procrastinate and take their time to sign on the dotted line.

Chloe tells me about one such client. She asks me what she might do to fix this situation. She's thought up a whole lot of imaginary reasons why this client isn't signing. She even makes assumptions on why the client doesn't want to sign with her — talking herself out of the sale.

I ask what she might ask her prospect to move things forward.

Chloe comes up with questions such as:

- "Do you need more details from me?"
- "Can I have a conversation with your business partners?"
- "Can I get another meeting with you and your whole team?"

If you notice, these are all closed questions. They're based on what Chloe thinks the next step might be. The meanest of clients might even say yes or no to them, which wouldn't help Chloe move forward. In fact, the door might close altogether if the answer is no.

An open question, meanwhile, might invite the client to really think. And, if Chloe were to ask an open question, it would give her the chance to really listen.

I ask Chloe if she can think of a more open question to ask. After some thought, she comes up with the following:

- "What do you need next?"
- "How might I help you with this?"

When Chloe stops asking closed questions based on the story she makes up in her mind — and when she lets go of needing to fix things — she is able to ask a genuinely open question. In turn, she can find out what her client is really thinking.

Open questions can help anyone understand another person's needs, wants, concerns and motivations.

A truly open question is one you don't know the answer to. It generates curiosity, and literally opens up the conversation. Asking open questions can also strengthen the relationship — the other person will see you as being genuinely interested in hearing more.

I'm sure you already know the difference between a closed and an open question. What, however, is the difference for you when you actually put open questions into your daily conversations?

PRACTICE

What is your ratio of closed-to-open questions?
If you're not sure, start listening to the questions you ask. Open questions start with How, What, When, Where or Why. What changes when you open up your questions?

25. THERE'S ALWAYS ANOTHER POSSIBILITY

"That's just how we do things around here." We've all heard this refrain before. There's also, "I don't have the authority to decide that," along with, "I'll have to ask my manager."

When your mind is fixed on an automatic or habituated stance, and you don't explore other possibilities, you may get stuck on an edge.

A fixed mindset can show up in pretty extreme ways. You might not always recognise how fixed you've made yourself. Here's one from my personal experience:

It is early on a dark and dreary Aberdeen morning. My husband and I have taken the same flight to our adopted home in Canada probably 20 times or more. We know the routine...or so I think.

At the check-in desk we learn that the airline has changed procedure. We will need to collect our own luggage at Heathrow and drag it through the long corridor adjoining Terminals 1 and 3. It's early morning, and I haven't eaten much breakfast.

My mind is closed. I'm incensed that we received no notification of this change, and insist that we won't have enough time to collect our luggage and make our connecting flight. In my mindset, this is going to be a disaster.

I keep repeating the same complaint. "We'll miss our connection." Through my agitation, I eventually hear the supervisor tell her check-in staff, "If that lady causes any more trouble, let me know and I'll call the police." I go silent as I realise she's talking about me.

The attendant finishes checking us in. I watch our suitcases disappear. As I quiet my mind, I open up to another possibility: the airline wouldn't have intentionally set us up to miss our connecting flight. There must be another way. Is it possible that this could work, and that I just can't see it?

In the end, it takes less than 12 minutes to collect our luggage and walk Heathrow's long corridor for our next flight. We make it with plenty of time.

Indeed, there *was* another way — I just couldn't see it. I had limited my belief in what was possible. When I shifted my perspective, I freed myself from my self-imposed angst, and recognised the other way this situation could unfold.

Sometimes, what seems impossible turns out to be the opposite. There are many more possibilities than you may at first allow yourself to see. Irish philosopher John O'Donohue (whose writing and poetry are a great source of inspiration to me) suggests that there are dozens of unseen possibilities if only we would look for them. "Where," he asks, "do all those other unused possibilities go?"

Asking 'What if?' or 'What will it take?' questions will shift stuck mindsets and reveal other possibilities to you and your team.

PRACTICE

Ask yourself and others, "What if there's another way?" Use this question to open your mind to what's possible, rather than focusing on what's wrong. Encourage others to explore what's possible to generate their own growth mindsets.

26. FOCUS FORWARD

The right question at the right time can move you closer to your desired outcome. A powerful question in the perfect moment can open up your mind, and reveal insights you haven't considered.

Some questions, though, take you backwards, especially when you feel you need to understand more about a situation before you can take action.

Questions that look backwards can feel comfortable. And, you can certainly argue that they're worth it. Yet, these questions can sometimes be time-consuming traps.

That's because the mind kicks into a certain kind of logic that says, "If only I knew the whole story, I'd be able to fix things." Take the following example, involving Joe:

As a manager, Joe likes to jump in and solve problems. He tends to phrase questions in ways that help him analyse what's wrong. For instance:

- "What's the problem?"
- "How did this happen?"
- "What have you done about this?"

These can be valid questions. However, as soon as Joe asks them, conversations go backwards. His team starts rehashing the situation, instead of looking forward. What's more, they don't consider these questions helpful. In fact, they hate bringing problems to Joe, since his questions either waste time, or make them feel worse about the situation.

Joe's questions often lead to simple, unfortunate conclusions.

He goes from criticism to judgment pretty quickly. And it doesn't take him long until he lands on dire consequences:

- "This employee always screws up."
- "I'm tired of fixing messes."
- "I need to replace this person."
- "It's this team member's fault."

How can Joe reframe his questions? Consider the types of questions that Mark, a leadership coach, likes to ask:

- "How is this impacting you?"
- "What will help you feel better about this situation?"
- "What does success look like, related to this situation?"
- "What do you need in order to reach your desired outcome?"
- "What would you rather create?"

Forward-looking questions help teams articulate their thoughts, and find options and opportunities to change or take action. They create positive momentum, move conversations forward, and encourage you to explore new possibilities together.

When you hear forward-looking questions you realise your ideas are more productive than you first thought. You can unlock new ideas that lurk just below the surface, and see the potential, rather than the problem. Everyone moves forward.

PRACTICE

Check your direction. Keep an eye on where your questions take other people. Are people gaining clarity and momentum? Are they stuck in the past? Or are they wandering around in a loop?

27. FROM CONFLICT TO CURIOSITY

The only problem with conflict is that we call it conflict. Think about it. If the word didn't exist, you might call conflict something less threatening, like 'differences', 'challenges', or simply 'perspectives'.

What if much of what you label as 'conflict' is the result of what happens when different perspectives, needs and wants converge?

This thing you call 'conflict' may only feel threatening because someone — perhaps you — wants to prove something, or win the argument over others.

When you realise that you might actually be the person creating conflict, you can reframe it and shift your stance.

This reminds me of my story from the airport check-in, a few practices ago. There was a situation I wasn't happy with, but in the end, I was the one creating the conflict.

I'm not talking about times when you're dealing with outright abuse, or even rudeness. In no way should you take those on as somehow being your fault. You also don't need to create conflict situations around them.

Indeed, in extreme circumstances, you are likely best to walk away carefully, and with your nature intact. (Please note that there are many complexities with real abuse situations. I'm not qualified here to address them. If you are in, or are aware of such a situation, please seek appropriate professional support.)

I'm speaking about the relatively innocuous conversations you might find yourself in, where you create the experience of conflict for yourself and others. Or, a situation you might label as a potential conflict, in order to avoid or escape it.

As much as we might hate to admit it, almost all of us do this from time to time.

One of the most common fears I hear in my coaching conversations is that people don't like conflict. Yet conflict is only a word. What you don't like is the feeling of being hurt, or of hurting others.

Drop the word/label 'conflict,' and free yourself from those imaginary fears. Instead of being confused by them, boldly proclaim, "I know this might make us both feel uncomfortable, but let's talk about it anyway to see where we can get to."

Allow yourself and the other person the grace and space to truly explore, then go where you must, and see what you might create beyond the conflict.

There's a world beyond the one you call conflict. It's called curiosity, and it starts with a question.

PRACTICE

Pretend the word 'conflict' no longer exists. Enter each conversation with the sense of what's possible. Put your trust in yourself and others to work through tensions that arise.

28. BE CURIOUS, NOT COMPLACENT

Today, I thought about how, in many cases, the majority of people are quite complacent with receiving answers, or being told what to do.

Upwards, people complain about what 'they' are imposing — meaning managers or 'the company'. I recall a workshop with a group of technical managers who kept saying 'they' need to communicate better. I asked repeatedly who 'they' were. It took almost half an hour for the penny to drop, and for the group to realise they were playing the victim: blaming the faceless company collective, rather than asking how each of them personally might in fact take a lead in demonstrating better communication.

In complacency, many people in organisations don't feel like they are entitled to ask questions.

Imagined fear can keep you quiet. It invokes your avoidance patterns. It makes you complacent — because to challenge anything is to create a problem, which provokes the fear of getting into trouble.

To break free of complacency, you might:

- Be more genuinely open to hearing, exploring, or expanding on ideas with others.
- Consider seeing each other as equal contributors.
- Ask yourself, "What's been my contribution to this situation? How might I take a different perspective?"

This is a two-way process. Lucy, a client of mine, recognises during one of our conversations that she often sits in judgement of both her team members and her leaders. She is frustrated that on both sides, they see the world differently from her. It results in a lot of stalemate, complaining and blame.

And yet, she hesitates to have real conversations with them. Instead she keeps spinning in her own perspectives and judgements.

We develop a series of questions for her to enter into conversations with more curiosity. These will help her discover ways to bring different perspectives together, and travel a more aligned path with her colleagues.

She becomes more curious to understand the world through their eyes, and to value and join their perspectives with her own. This ultimately creates something new she hadn't seen before.

She starts to feel much better about other people — and about herself.

Ultimately, mutual growth happens. Curiosity uncovers more for everyone, and moves people from complacent acceptance to creative action.

PRACTICE

Be more curious to see the world from others' perspectives.
Notice if you are stuck in acceptance, or even blame. Ask yourself: "How am I contributing to this situation?" What can you change to create a different outcome?

29. PLAY EDGY, NOT SAFE

If you want to always feel safe, you are unlikely to explore the edges where breakthroughs, learning and growth await.

You may be familiar with the phrase, "This is a safe space." How many of us have stopped to consider the fact that creating a safe space actually comes from feeling:

- Unsafe
- Hurt
- Offended
- Afraid to offend others

This is the bane of today's politically correct mindset. We can see all around us how it's leading to ineffectual conversations. We're almost at the point where it's hardly 'safe' to say anything.

In 2015, Google identified psychological safety as one of the keys to a successful team. They defined it as meaning people were "able to take risks on this team without feeling insecure or embarrassed."

Sometimes my coaching clients will say things like, "I don't feel comfortable." They hold back from speaking up in meetings, or among colleagues at work — which in turn holds them back.

Some years ago, when working with a client leadership team, we uncovered an *aha* moment between two senior leaders. Brenda was walking past the company's reception building, and noticed the windows were dirty. She had the thought that it didn't create a very good impression for first-time visitors. Brenda hesitated, however, to mention it to her colleague in charge of the reception building, not wanting to seem like she was criticising or offending her.

Playing it safe, Brenda missed the chance to improve the company's image, and inadvertently let herself and others down.

This feels like a real edge for many people. Do you play safe? Or do you feel you can take some risks when it will make a difference? What really holds you back from the edge?

Remember: as you hold yourself back, you also hold back the chance at improvement, growth, and solving challenges.

Feelings of fear do not need to stop you. Instead of seeing them as roadblocks, think of them as radar signals that warn you things might be uncomfortable. Don't turn away. Go toward them.

Quite often, what follows is an essential conversation.

PRACTICE

Got to your edge. Say what's on your mind (in a courteous manner, of course). Respect the other person enough to be honest with the best of intentions. In the process, you'll help each other grow, learn and make a difference.

30. DREAM BIG

What if I told you that your conversations can be the opening to the big dreams that create your future? This is the very premise of coaching conversations.

In fact, my mantra for many of my clients is: "Dream Big, Live Fully, Lead Boldly."

There have been so many times when I've witnessed a client speak their dreams aloud, and bring their ambitions to a coaching conversation. Sure enough, these instances become catalytic moments when clients realise what they want, and start believing they can make it real.

Your dream may seem so big that you're scared to give voice to it. In conversation with the right people — parents, teachers, mentors, coaches, partners, and any-one you feel is 'on your side' — I advocate speaking aloud what you believe, even if you feel it's not yet within your grasp.

To hear yourself say your dream aloud is to help yourself create it. I encourage my coaching clients to live fully into their dreams, as if the dream is already real.

Years ago I worked with a young manager whose position in the company came to an end. We were exploring what he might want to do next. Initially, there didn't appear to be an automatic fit for him in the organisation. Instead, we talked about his dreams for himself and for his family. He envisaged working abroad, giving his children a different life of opportunity.

Yet, he kept saying things like, "That's not going to happen. I'd like to work and live in Australia or Canada, but the company doesn't even have offices in either place."

The more he heard himself say what he wanted, the more his desire to create it strengthened. Even though it seemed impossible, he heard himself speaking more strongly about the experience of life in a new country.

Hearing himself say it led to new conversations with his company, where he let them know what he wanted. Eventually, his dream came true.

Within one year of our coaching conversation, he emailed to say his company was opening an office overseas. They'd invited him to be the manager.

Conversation can be the place where you dream big, and open yourself up to what's possible. First, though, you must hear yourself say what you really want.

PRACTICE

Your favourite question today will be 'WHAT IF?'
Use this question to share your dreams with others.
Then, ask them what dreams they've been keeping quiet.

CLARITY

CLARITY

"As individuals, as organisations, and as an entire species, clarity is the key to solving the big issues that face us if we want to create a sustainable future for ourselves and the generations that follow us."

— JAMIE SMART, *The Little Book of Clarity*

"I need clarity," is something I hear a lot. It's often used as an excuse for not taking action. "I need to be clear first," is what many clients will say.

Yet, if I'm out for dinner one evening, and upon leaving the restaurant, I discover that a North Sea fog has descended and completely blanketed the world around me, I won't wait for clarity before I set off toward home.

I'll get in my car, and start to make my way.

There's that little space just beyond the reach of my car headlights, where I can see far enough to move carefully along, bit by bit, one short distance at a time.

Focusing, I eventually make it home — perhaps only a few minutes later than if I'd rushed along the highway on a clear night.

The practices at this fourth edge of conversation will keep you moving forward, one piece of clarity at a time, as you:

- keep reaching just beyond where you can see…
- feel your way through confusions or misunderstandings…
- and create a path, step by step, for your journey.

Stepping into the fog is the only way to find the clarity you seek.

In speaking with others, the conversation moves forward as you express each word, thought or idea. As each next question or suggestion comes to light, the fog or confusion gradually lifts around you.

Quite suddenly, you find yourself closer to home than if you had waited for all the fog to clear before you said a thing.

31. FROM SHOULD TO WANT

Jenny is a senior leader in an entrepreneurial company. Together, we've been developing a culture that encourages and equips everyone to lead conversations that make a difference. Our aim is for everyone to have a hand in the company moving forward.

Jenny wants to know how she might best respond to someone who comes and asks, "What do you think I should do about XYZ?"

She's tried a few approaches, including waiting to give an answer. She wants to discover other ways to respond to this type of request.

A cynic might suggest that any team member who asks this type of question is being lazy, and wants the leader to give them the answer.

If Jenny were to provide the answer straight off, she'd be conditioning employees to rely on her whenever they need direction. And, she'd be taking time away from her own priorities.

When you're busy solving everyone else's situations, you never have time to solve your own.

Working together, Jenny and I come up with a plan. She'll answer such a question with one of her own:

"What do you want to do?"

This sounds very different to Jenny from the *should* question her team member asked.

When *should* shows up in a question, it may be a sign that someone either wants to please you, doesn't want responsibility, or is afraid to get something wrong.

When you give in to these questions, and tell your team what you think they should do, you take away whatever power they have. You also miss an opportunity to help them grow.

Instead, by asking "What do you want to do?" you show up as a leader who believes in the other person, and wants to help them unlock their ideas.

You invite team members into conversations that move ideas forward, and you encourage them to work things out for themselves.

When a team member can find a solution, they'll feel better about their contribution. Instead of just doing what the leader thinks, they can be creative, and even grow.

PRACTICE

When people ask, "What do you think I SHOULD do?" reply with, "What do you WANT to do?" Give them time to think, and help them take their next step.

32. PRESS PAUSE

If you were to apply only one or two practices from this book, I invite you to include this one. There are so many reasons why it makes sense to create more pauses in your life. It could involve giving yourself a chance to refresh on holiday, getting home earlier to put the kids to bed, or putting your cellphone in your pocket so you can look straight ahead as you walk.

Within each conversation, there's a moment to press pause and, as my granny used to say, remember to think before you speak.

Recently, I forgot my own advice and put my foot in it, speaking without thinking on what might have turned out to be a very delicate situation.

I went to drop something off at the doctor's office. It was just after 9 a.m., a time when the waiting room is usually choc-a-block with patients. This time, a solitary senior sat amidst empty chairs.

It was like someone had pressed pause. I found myself waiting for some unseen finger to press the play button again, and set things whirling back into action.

Without thinking, I joked with the young receptionist, "Very quiet in here. Don't you have any doctors today?"

She smiled gently at my remark.

"No," she said. "They've all gone to a funeral of someone very close to us."

I could have kicked myself. Had I pressed pause before speaking, I might have worked out the fact that there would indeed be an important reason for the waiting room to be so empty.

A coaching conversation is, in itself, a time to pause your thinking. When clients come to a coaching conversation feeling stressed, angry or anxious, the first thing I suggest is for them to take a deep breath, then press pause. I want them to hear themselves and contemplate what's really going on in their head and heart.

If life is a movie, then this practice gives you the button to:

- Stop, rewind and pay closer attention.
- Consider more consciously what you want or need.
- Shift the conversation, or change the channel altogether.

There's a quote attributed to Klaus Schwab, Executive Chairman of the World Economic Forum, which considers the speed of today's technology:

"As the novelty of wearable tech gives way to necessity — and, later, as wearable tech becomes embedded tech — will we be deprived of the chance to pause, reflect, and engage in meaningful, substantive conversations? How will our inner lives and ties to those around us change?"

Pressing pause more often now can only prepare us for an even faster world on the way.

PRACTICE

Press pause before you speak. Ask a question, or comment on something you see or hear. Notice how small nuances shift the meaning of the whole experience.

33. ASK "WHAT DO YOU NEED?"

"What do you need?" I asked my mother a few months after my father's death left her grieving and alone.

"I don't know what I need," she answered.

The question is rarely asked, yet without it, you're eager to offer what you think someone needs.

When I was attending evening classes for my professional HR qualification (many years ago now) I recall being introduced to Maslow's Hierarchy of Needs. I loved how the tutor described it, and the beautiful triangle she drew on the blackboard. Then I thought to myself, "Will I ever use this?" It seemed like it was just a theory, and I wasn't sure of its practical use or application.

Little did I know that Maslow's hierarchy would inform one of the most important questions I ask in my life's work. Asking it brings a client's awareness to what he or she truly needs, and creates a powerful conversation.

The question "What do you need?" often stops people in their tracks. They fear they'll come across as needy or demanding. As such, they might respond with "I need to…" which is another way of saying "I should…"

Notice some differences:

- Question: "What do you need?"
- Answer: "I need more authority to make decisions." This is an expression of a true need.

Meanwhile:

- Question: "What do you need?"
- Answer: "I need to get this finished." This is essentially a 'should' statement, not a request for something to enhance your role.

Asking for, and expressing true needs, takes conversations to deeper, more intimate, and more meaningful levels.

I sometimes hesitate to ask coaching clients what they really need. What if their needs are too challenging, demanding, or downright scary? Then I remember that my job is to get them to express their needs, and watch them grow in self-belief and confidence.

If you want to grow your team, your business, or your home life, take time to ask "What do you need?" Doing so will uncover the varying levels of need sitting under the surface.

Expressing curiosity about people's real needs can create increased awareness of what's truly important to each person at this point in their life and work.

PRACTICE

Ask, "What do you need?"
Take care to create space after asking it.
Give the other person time to think about how to fulfil that need.

34. WHOSE AGENDA IS IT ANYWAY?

I love when groups come to a workshop, and someone says, "I'll keep an open mind."

How often do we carry our own agenda into a room or situation, determined to fulfil it? I can't help but wonder: Is it possible to have a truly open mind?

I'm convinced that a truly open mind is impossible when you consider the amount of background noise that teems between our ears every time we step into a conversation.

Does that mean we should quit trying to bring open minds into situations? No.

We can be aware of the noise, along with any agenda that the noise pulls us toward.

We can put the agenda aside, even for a short while, in order to fully participate in the conversation in front of us, and be genuinely open to the perspectives that others bring.

If we stay attached to our agenda only, we might as well just have the conversation with ourselves. Imagine a world filled with lots of people muttering alone in corners!

When we're in a conversation, the intent is to listen to the many aspects that the other person brings forward. Then, we can build on each aspect, and work toward things like:

- a deeper understanding
- a more comprehensive appreciation of perspectives
- a stronger connection and relationship
- a mutual path that leads to better solutions

Remember: the meaning of the word 'conversation' is a manner of behaving together with others.

When you're open to others, you'll discover what's beyond your own fixed agenda.

PRACTICE

Set aside your own agenda by listening to others.
If you are the leader, put your agenda on the table last.

35. SAY "I HEAR YOU"

This is an easy one — not just on paper, but in practice too.

I've mentioned already how I like to listen to certain podcasts. Recently I was listening to Sam Harris.

His guest had a particular habit of repeating each of Harris' questions slowly before answering.

It seemed like he was taking time to ponder the question.

By repeating it, he also gave Harris the opportunity to confirm it was in fact the question he had asked.

How useful might this be as a practice?

First, you repeat the question. Secondly, you use additional affirmations that confirm what you've heard.

Three such affirmations come to mind:

- "I hear you."
- "That's a great question, let me think about that for a moment." (I hear this often from clients.)
- "I've never thought of that before."

These are simple yet powerful ways to help you focus into the conversation, to take time to really hear something, and to affirm that you've absorbed the question you've just heard.

PRACTICE

Repeat questions out loud as you contemplate your response. Use phrases like "I hear you," or "That's a great question," before speaking.

36. DON'T LUMP US ALL TOGETHER

"If only he'd stop referring to us as THEM," says my rather stressed-out client.

"He lumps us all together as if we all think and act the same, need the same things, and have the same challenges. It's as if he thinks we're a one-size-fits-all group. I'd like him to refer to me as an individual — even to use my name more often."

My client's complaint is about a classic 'leader-speak' default position: to use the collective instead of the individual. In one word, this contradicts any intention a leader might have to create an empowered and accountable culture.

When there's little or no individual recognition, people don't feel heard or appreciated for their efforts and contributions.

I know it sounds trivial — maybe even like I'm splitting hairs. Yet, consider this: What if stopping the 'THEM' talk proves to be one of the simplest, most powerful ways to improve your conversations?

Yes, I agree there are such things as group conversations. However, even within a group, individuals bring unique voices.

Imagine, as a leader, you're in a meeting. You ask each person to express his or her opinion. Instead of hearing "I think…" or "in my opinion…" you're met with a steady stream of "they think…" or "the team says…"

Unless you receive a clear indication that everyone on the team thinks exactly the same thing — and I don't know what such an indication would be — then what you'd be experiencing is a breakdown of the individual voice, for the sake of a summary.

If this isn't what you asked for, would you be happy?

Now imagine the other side. Your people want to know that you see and recognise them for their individual contributions. How does each person feel every time you bundle them together?

Forcing everyone into a group is a super-powerful habit that anyone can change. To do so, start referring to specific people by their names:

- "In the meeting, I heard Aileen say…"
- "Joan, Jack and Bill agreed about…"
- "I loved the way Mark stood up for himself when…"

This small change shows that you've heard every contribution, and that you respect each of them. It also brings listening to a deeper and more connected level.

We live in a world of generalisations. It's all too easy to jump to group conclusions on the basis of one person's words or actions.

Generalisations can lead us away from real connections. Great conversations require that we honour each person's voice, and see each other for the value we contribute.

PRACTICE

Catch yourself when you lump people together.
Refer to each person you're talking with, and not the group as a whole.

37. THE POWER OF 'I'

Take a listen around you. Notice how often people deflect and shy away from speaking in the 'I' voice, and opt instead for the more global 'we'.

- We're too old for this.
- We've got this wrong.
- We don't think like that around here.
- We've always done it this way.

Is there a societal fear around speaking in the 'I'? There may well be.

There's an unspoken assumption that using 'I' comes across as arrogant, egotistical, bossy, or overpowering.

I hold the opposite view. I encourage clients to speak in the 'I' voice. I want them to really feel, own and explore what they're trying to say. I often reiterate that it's okay to speak as 'I'.

The tone of 'I' conveys power, confidence, and conviction. It says:

- I stand in my truth.
- I have presence.
- I own my words.
- I need to be heard.

There's a legacy from the 1970s, particularly in a business context, where it's assumed that being a team means speaking as 'we'. And there's the work of Judith Glaser, and the WE Institute, that emphasises how we are all connected.[13]

Even if that is the case, we can only connect with each other after we first recognise ourselves as individuals.

I'm surprised how many leaders still buy into overplaying the 'we', or eschewing the 'I' altogether. I understand the desire to build teamwork and consensus, but I believe that using 'I' is the way to do so.

When you drop down to the generic 'we', you run the risk of making everyone feel like their ideas will get lost in the shuffle, rather than rise to the top.

People use 'we' to keep themselves safe. As a leader, you can model the use of 'I', and encourage others to speak up and bring their bold ideas to the fore. This can spark more ideas, and help you discover what each person feels and thinks.

Contrary to the glib adage that there is no 'I' in team, I believe there are ONLY 'I's in any team. That way, the team can recognise each person's unique contribution, and embrace the sum of every 'I' working together.

PRACTICE

Use 'I' more often when speaking.
Listen for and encourage the unique 'I' voice in each person you talk with.

38. UN-JUMBLE YOUR QUESTIONS

It's confusing when someone asks a question, then asks a follow-up question before the other person has time to answer the FIRST question. For instance:

"How's work going today?"
"Well..."
"What are you up to around 11:30?"
"Let me..."
"What time are you taking lunch?"

How can I know which of these questions the other person wants me to answer, or even cares about?

When you ask a jumble of questions, it's not clear what you're really asking, or wishing to achieve. This creates serious disconnect, which will not help you build a connection.

The best I can do is to answer what I think I've heard, or give an answer that's based on how I interpret what someone is asking. Invariably, we'll have to go over things at least once more. Why? One of two reasons:

• The other person didn't ask me directly what he or she really wanted to know.
• The answer I gave didn't satisfy what he or she really wanted to hear.

There's something else to consider: When you ask a jumble of questions, the other person's brain is consumed with trying to work out what you're asking. It's almost impossible to focus on providing a quality answer.

Sadly, this often passes as conversation. It's also where we waste a lot of time, get frustrated, talk over each other, and walk away feeling incomplete or misunderstood.

Why do we jumble questions? I believe it's because we're overly concerned about whether we're asking the right question in the right way. We repeat the same question, but a slightly altered version. By doing so, we hope to clarify what we're asking.

To be on the receiving end of this kind of barrage can be like having a stiff wind in your face when you're just trying to walk down the street.

Be brave. Ask one question and wait for an answer. If your listener doesn't 'get' what you're asking, they'll let you know. Only then can you re-word your question in order to clarify.

PRACTICE

Ask one clear question at a time. Wait for an answer.

39. ASKING PERMISSION

In *Quiet Leadership*, David Rock introduces the concept of asking permission before you:

- Share something new, delicate or challenging.
- Pivot toward a difficult or different topic.

Rock suggests that if we want someone to enter into a meaningful conversation, we might invite their explicit permission to get personal, or to go deeper.

If conversation is truly a dance, then everyone must be willing to move together with the tune. That includes moments when the tempo changes, or when a new band takes the stage.

One fundamental premise of coaching is that a coach doesn't impose his or her ideas or solutions on a client. We facilitate clients as they arrive at their own solutions. This might be THE ONE thing that creates a different feel to coaching-style conversations. And, I believe that everyone could benefit from adopting a similar approach. Rather than telling others what to do, support them as they discover answers.

Like Rock's idea above, coaches ask permission before suggesting something, or sharing new ideas with a client. What does asking permission do?

- It brings people's attention to what you are about to say.
- It shows respect for the other person.
- It gives both parties a chance to catch their breath.
- It helps you focus on what you really want to say.
- It makes seemingly hard conversations much easier.

- It strengthens and deepens relationships.
- It helps set boundaries for what's on and off the table.
- It infuses conversations with etiquette and politeness.
- It builds trust.
- It can help you solve problems, and change the energy of a moment when people are in conflict or opposition.

Permission is an interesting thing these days.

In some cases, people feel like they can't do anything unless they're told to. Conversely, lots of people breach the rules because they feel like they don't need permission.

In this practice, I'm talking about polite permission that follows a gentle track in the midst of a conversation:

- "Are you open to hearing more about X?"
- "May I share something with you that's a little off-topic?"
- "Can I ask a quick follow-up question?"

There are definitely people who don't feel like they need permission. They're sure that they possess the right to say what they want, when they want, to whomever they wish. When dealing with them, how can any of us be inspired to share our ideas?

If you're this person, think about all of the things that others are choosing NOT to share with you.

PRACTICE

Focus on asking gentle permission before you ask a tricky question, or share new ideas. Pay attention to how permission works when you encounter a difficult or challenging situation. In the process, you'll help each other grow, learn, and make a difference.

COMPLETION

COMPLETION

"That was a great conversation."

— NUMEROUS COACHING CLIENTS

I love hearing those words at the end of a coaching conversation. I take a moment to acknowledge them, and also to reflect on what it was that made the conversation so great.

As I touched upon earlier, the reason why many clients walk away with this impression is because they have not experienced conversations that feel so complete before.

Is it possible for more conversations to end with this great feeling? Not just coaching conversations, but those we have throughout the day with coworkers, leaders, family members, spouses, and even strangers?

This final edge in the arc of conversation — completion — holds many of our earlier practices together.

It's not about being nice, or even being happy.

It's about:

- Feeling that the conversation has served a meaningful purpose.
- Connecting with each other in a meaningful way.
- Caring enough to listen, and to be heard fully.
- Staying open to what emerges throughout the conversation through a shared sense of curiosity, and the willingness to open new doors.

When multiple parties agree that the conversation feels complete, it's a sign that you've moved together, step by step and word by word, through whatever fog or confusion might have existed. When you arrive at the end of the conversation, you share the sense that it was all worth it.

The practices at this final edge in the arc are intended to ensure that you pay attention to how you end your conversations. Don't just walk away from each other, either in anger or in joy. Instead, pay close attention to the final moments.

It's similar to the way credits roll at the end of a movie. A lot of people get up as soon as the film finishes to rush out of the cinema. Other people take their time, relish in the movie's impact, and hold on to certain emotions a bit longer.

At this final edge of conversation, I urge you to linger.

Doing so can create space so you and others can ask key questions, and/or check that the conversation is in a good place. Waiting can also help you reflect on what the conversation really means for you. What have you learned, gained and experienced? How might you feel changed?

Finally, just like a movie's credits, you can use the extra time to acknowledge and thank each other for contributing to the great conversation.

Many conversations are greater than we take time to acknowledge.

When you've mapped out what makes your conversations great, you'll be equipped to make your way back to more great conversations again and again, especially when you know the senses of satisfaction and fulfilment that are waiting.

You might even become slightly addicted to great conversations and want to work in this field, as I am honoured to do.

40. KEEP IT SHORT

It's my theory that the most powerful and impactful questions are short, perhaps no more than five-words long. Let's test it. Consider the distinction between these two questions:

1. "Do you think you could take the lead and show the team what results are needed from this project?"

VS:

2. "How will you lead this?"

The first question is typical of the way many questions are framed these days.

- It's a closed question. The recipient could just answer Yes or No without consideration. Then, the questioner would have to move the idea forward.

- It's also a leading question. The questioner has simply suggested what needs to happen. It's instruction disguised as asking.

- It offers no ownership or engagement, nor does it suggest that the questioner believes the other person can come up with a solution.

- The questioner doesn't show any curiosity or interest in how the other person wants to respond. The question simply asks whether the other person thinks she can take on the job. It doesn't open up space for her to communicate 'how' she will do so. This is a common habit for many people.

- It's so wordy that it sucks all the air out of any potential conversation. The recipient might feel pressured to respond with a quick Yes or No. Or, she might get lost trying to decipher what the question means.

It's a quick exchange that passes for conversation between meetings, and assumes that the people involved understand each other — whether or not that's true.

Now consider the shorter version:

- It conveys genuine interest and curiosity on what approach the other person will take.
- It demonstrates that the questioner trusts that the other person is capable of considering the question.
- It encourages the recipient to stop and think. This increases ownership, engagement and accountability.
- It is reflective of a leader who doesn't need to have all the answers, or show that her answers are always right.
- It shows that she cares about other people's thoughts.

- It invites new thinking, ideas and solutions.
- It generates deeper layers of conversation. With space to consider the answer, the recipient will more likely respond with a similarly short and curious question. The conversation can evolve, bringing more layers of meaning and understanding to light.

It makes life easier in the long run, as it shows others how to ask questions that open up deeper thinking. Recipients grow more self-reliant. They no longer have to lean on the leader for all of the answers.

When people begin to see that their thoughts, ideas and opinions are invited, they become more prepared to express and share.

PRACTICE

Formulate short, clear questions, then ask them.
Start with What, How, Where, When, or even Why.

41. FILL IN THE BLANKS

'Communication' and 'conversation' are not the same thing. We readily use the word 'communication' in business. When you look at what the word actually describes, you see a one-way process in which a person conveys information or data that they think another person should know.

In my day, corporate executives would hold 'town hall' meetings, which essentially meant they stood on stage and spoke at their audience. When they asked for any questions, there was usually silence. Audience members would often leave having misinterpreted most of what they heard.

Today, emerging and interactive technologies encourage audience members to ask questions, and to essentially create more dialogue, even in large group settings. And the name has changed from 'town hall' to 'all-hands' events.

What people choose to hear is not always what the speaker means to convey.

Creating more space for questions and exchanging ideas will minimise and clarify the blanks, even if you can't control what people choose to hear.

However, you can take steps to minimise the blank space where people make up their own answers and stories. How? By moving from communication to conversation.

Conversation invites others to explore and confirm what they think they heard, in order to get to the bottom of what you actually said.

In a conversation, you can take time to unpack the interpretations that others put on your message and words. And, you can begin to understand where their responses come from.

I call this: Filling in the blanks, and completing the conversation.

PRACTICE

Do not leave conversations with unasked questions, or with unaddressed misunderstandings. Check that the conversation is complete before walking away.

42. BE ENOUGH

Marisa Peer, a world-renown speaker, Rapid Transformational Therapy trainer, and best-selling author, says that everything in life boils down to one thing: Feeling that you are enough. She claims that even her richest, most successful, most famous clients carry this underlying doubt that they are not enough.

They turn to her because they can't understand how even with all their trappings of wealth and success, they still don't feel good about themselves.

Like me, you probably 'get' that money doesn't make happiness. Yet (again like me), your life is likely structured around the pursuit of various forms of wealth and security.

One of my favourite coaching conversations is to explore the following two-part question:

- "When will you have and be enough?"
- "When will you know you've reached that point?"

Many organisational and society structures are designed around feelings of not being enough:

- You're not top of the class.
- You're not promoted.
- There's never enough money in the budget to invest.
- There aren't enough sales.
- You're not fit, healthy enough, etc.

Yet, in a semantic twist, all of what we have, do and experience IS good enough. For the majority of people it's good enough to put food on the table, to clothe their children, and to find satisfying work.

Your mind chooses whether you live in the 'good enough' or the 'not good enough' space. The conversations you create are a reflection of where you are on the 'enough' spectrum.

Performance reviews are based on feeling like we're 'not good enough'. We're told to stretch our skills, produce, and help create growth. However, growth cannot be exponential and never-ending. At some point, it has to 'be enough'.

The natural cycle for anything is the same: it grows to a point, then it dies. If you keep over-feeding, you'll end its life.

This cycle is replicated in many of our systems and structures. Let it not be so in our conversations.

It might seem contradictory, but the more you focus on where you are good enough, the stronger, more capable, and more positive you will feel about what you might achieve in your life.

Now imagine how impactful it will be if we focus and build on what's enough in conversations. Can you feel your chest puff out and your eyes widen as you realise how 'enough-ness' gives you energy to take one step further?

Here's a quote from Charles Duhigg: "If you tell people that they have what it takes to succeed, they'll prove you right." That's because, like you, they are enough!

PRACTICE

Be enough. Do enough. Say enough. Live enough.
Let others know they are enough.
Enjoy the enough-ness.

43. TRUST YOUR TRUTH

When I did my TEDx talk in 2016, I didn't start out with a clear message or idea that I wanted to spread, as the intention behind TED and TEDx requires. Instead, I wanted to see if I could get on stage, and discover how the experience might go from there.

When I'm coaching, I want to engage people in conversation. I prefer to engage with an audience the same way.

I'm not interested in talking at people. Still, perhaps it was one step too far to think I might coach an entire TEDx audience.

I practiced with my coach, and his initial feedback was pretty direct:

"It's boring, Aileen."

How could I do things differently, and create a 12-minute conversation with an audience?

We decided that I would role-play a conversation that many in the audience would be familiar with: when someone wants to 'speak their truth' to their manager, but hesitates for fear of retribution.

I might mention that this approach meant twice the work for me. I had to learn and remember both sides of a conversation, which was much harder than simply speaking to the audience, and using a slide deck for visual support.

As it turns out, my 12 minutes flew by like some kind of out-of-body moment. I drew some laughs, and my posse of friends and family cheered me on.[14]

Maybe everyone secretly hopes their talk will go viral. Mine got a mild degree of interest. In the end, it was about trusting myself to do it more than anything.

This reminds me of something essential to completion: Speaking up and saying what you really think, whether on stage, at home or in the office, is a challenge. What's more, doing so without worrying about what others will think or say about you is where you encounter one of the most vital conversation edges.

The intention, or 'truth' of my talk, was to demonstrate that it didn't need to be a talk at all.

When you trust yourself to speak your truth, you will often be surprised, gratified and thrilled with the outcome. You'll discover that stepping up to the edge isn't as scary as you might have thought.

One piece my TEDx talk doesn't show is that the other person in the conversation has an unspoken truth as well. When you speak your truth, it also invites others to do the same — even if the other is your manager.

PRACTICE

When you hesitate to speak your truth, take a deep breath and go for it. Start with something like, "I don't know if you're willing to hear this, but..." or even "I really need to say this..." Trust yourself and your audience.

44. COMPLETE THE CONVERSATION

The words of the song "Walk Away Renee"[15] come into my head as I sit to write this practice. Except, instead of hearing the actual lyrics ("just walk away, Renee"), I swap in the word 'don't' for 'just,' thereby changing the entire meaning. Now, the singer is telling Renee NOT to walk away, instead of encouraging her to do so.

What does this have to do with completion? Well, at the crux of the concept — and its greater place in the conversation edge — is the fact that many of us walk away before conversations are complete.

A lot of things get in the way of completing conversations.

Maybe there's another meeting to get to. Or perhaps we have other things on our minds. One of my clients says this about the busy-ness in his office: "We're getting lots of things done half-well, rather than getting fewer things done really well."

And so it goes with conversations that wind up as nothing more than fleeting words exchanged in haste. Do you find yourself moving on to the next meeting or activity, even while you're still processing the conversation from a moment ago? Does this suggest completeness, or the opposite?

When we walk away from conversations too soon — or when another person walks away too soon — we are left regretting not having taken the extra time to get there. We wind up carrying a stray, unshared thought without knowing what to do with it. "Note to self: email Suzie with an additional idea on how we might solve problem X."

When you're stuck on your last conversation, your attention can't move to the conversation that's happening now.

Sometimes, you might walk away because you want to remove yourself from a conversation. It's too challenging, or it's uncomfortable. You don't know what to say, and you're afraid of losing your composure. Or you're tired, drained…or bored.

I'm not an athletic person. I don't have the dedication and commitment it takes to push to the next level of physical performance. Yet, a friend who is an excellent skier once taught me that the only way to get beyond the pain point is to stretch your muscles just a little farther, or a bit longer. That way, the body learns to do more, regardless of what the mind says.

In any physical exercise, growth happens when you begin to trust the idea that the more you practice, the farther you go.

And so it is with conversation practices. The more you practice them, you begin to see where conversations will take you. If you can stay with a conversation one moment longer, you might be surprised by what you learn about yourself and your capacity to reach the next level.

PRACTICE

Make a point of staying in your conversations for a few minutes longer. Instead of asking "Are we done?" ask, "What more is there to say?" You might be surprised!

45. LEAVE IN INTEGRITY

I thought I understood the meaning of integrity. Isn't it about following through on your promises and commitments, doing what you say you'll do, and not letting people down?

Yes, it's all of these thing. And, as I discover during a master coaching class, there's another important spin to put on integrity that starts with this question:

What does it mean to be in integrity with yourself?

Look at how I define integrity above. Now, change things around a bit. To be in integrity with yourself means to:

- Not let yourself down.
- Follow through on the commitments you make to yourself.
- Do what you tell yourself you'll do.

This is also what it means to be fully accountable: to know that you do not question yourself, and that you are solid in your commitments, words and actions.

When I'm out of integrity with myself, I'm liable to say something like, "I'll finish my book by August," even when I know that's not going to happen. I'm just saying the words and hoping that somehow the book will write itself.

When I'm in integrity with myself, I truly hear when I say I will write for one hour each day. If I don't, then I'm letting myself down. Worse, I'm creating a situation where my words lack meaning. If they don't mean something to me, how can they mean something to anyone else?

Integrity is when something becomes non-negotiable. No distractions, excuses, or avoidance. Just pure, solid commitment to follow through on a promise.

If I don't live with integrity of self, why would anyone else do so for me?

As we approach the book's last few practices, I wonder if you might reflect on how integrity has played out for you thus far:

- Did you page through the book and say that maybe it would be good to try these practices one day?
- Have you focused on one practice at a time? How did it go?
- How serious are you about sustaining the learning and the practices you've used so far?
- How will you sustain your conversational progress as you go on from this book?

As you consider the differences that these practices have made in conversations, I have one more question:

Do these changes transfer over to the conversations you have with yourself?

At the end of the day, your inner conversations might be the most powerful conversations of all.

PRACTICE

Consider what being in full self-integrity means? Where has your integrity slipped ever so slightly? Did you do what you said you'd do for yourself today?

46. CATCH THE UNSAID

Conversations aren't merely the sum of what's spoken. They include layers that lie in a place called 'the unsaid'. As in many adventure stories, in that darkness is where we'll find treasure.

The unsaid might be explored through facial expressions, tone of voice, or body movements such as shrugs, folded arms or jumping out of the chair. It's also present in the silence between words and actions.

Left unsaid and un-named, these elements of conversation often end up in the world of assumptions.

For instance: She jumps out of her chair! Why?

- Is it 'for joy'? Could it have been excitement?
- Is she anxious about something? Impatient?
- Maybe she just remembered something she needs to do.

In the end, her actions might have nothing at all to do with our assumptions.

The unsaid elements of conversation lead us into the world of believing we know someone well enough to interpret and understand them without words.

That might be true in some deeply connected partnerships. However, it's rare for a work relationship to reach that depth of connection, even when we think we know someone's mind.

I often meet leaders who believe it is their job to 'understand' people. In reality, what they mean is they make interpretations and assumptions about people in order to work out the right way to manage them, believing they have worked out the unsaid and unspoken in another person.

Rather than trying to work people out in advance, you can deepen conversation by noticing the unsaid elements.

This starts by observing and listening beyond the words. It can be very honouring when you notice someone's distress, joy, or another signal that suggests there's something else going on. Noticing such things encompasses the arc of conversations outlined throughout this book, and demonstrates that:

- You're connected enough to notice something unsaid or unspoken.
- You care enough to check in and ask what's happening for them (rather than assuming or interpreting with your amateur psychology degree).
- You're curious enough to ask what's coming up for them.
- You get clear on their actual experience, not what you think their experience might be.
- You're able to have a complete conversation by giving voice to the unsaid.

This practice may well be one of the most important in the entire book. When the unsaid is named, it will either take you into a new world of ideas and solutions, or usher you into and beyond the world of 'I don't know'.

PRACTICE

Listen beyond words, being sure to observe what might otherwise be left unsaid.
Ask, "What remains unsaid here?"

47. TAKE TIME TO SUMMARISE

For most of the time I've worked with clients and organisations, the thing that people are MOST concerned about is how often they wind up literally running to meetings.

I asked a client recently how he manages it. Does he transport himself *Star Trek* style from the meeting that ends at 10 a.m. to the one that starts at 10 a.m.?

It's common to hear about people rushing from one meeting to the next with no time to think in between topics.

Surely, a lot of good thinking time, and agreed-upon actions, get lost as your mind switches instantly to a new topic. You tuck away the last meeting, make some brief notes, and hope that you'll remember the outcomes, not to mention what you promised or took on as next steps.

Do you see how this can cause extra effort and wasted energy?

Turns out, my client does not teleport to meetings. What he has learnt instead is to keep meetings to 50 minutes maximum. This gives people — and himself — time to breathe, reflect, put action items into place, or even get a cup of coffee or tea. Only then does he move on to the next meeting.

Can such a shift lead to more productive, creative and useful meetings? I think it could be that simple.

As soon as my client shortened his meetings, his manager began shortening his meetings too. Now, it's a common practice across his team.

Our effort increases to fill the time available.

If a meeting is scheduled for an hour, many people will sit there for an hour even if it's not productive. (Note: it's perfectly okay to leave a meeting if you feel you're neither contributing to, or gaining value from it. In fact, I coach clients to do so, especially if they know they can be more productive elsewhere. Of course, this type of exit conversation can be an edge that some people have difficulty approaching.)

One way to improve the effectiveness and impact of your conversations, no matter the setting, is to take time to summarise.

Summarising is a way to complete conversations, and check for understandings, actions and commitments.

I don't mean just summarising what you think was said, or what you think you said. It's more impactful to hear and understand what each person takes away from a conversation.

Before you wrap up a meeting, make time for each voice to be heard. Often, what gets declared is also what gets done. From that standpoint, taking a moment to summarise is a great way to strengthen accountability.

PRACTICE

Before meetings or conversations end, ask people to summarise their takeaways. Watch how they feel when they get to sum up and commit to next steps.

48. ASK FOR FEEDBACK

Many years ago I picked up a tool from a leadership program in San Francisco, that has proven one of the most useful tools I know. It is a way to receive, respond to and actually seek feedback.

First, I'm presuming that, like most people, you don't really like the word 'feedback'. You're not always comfortable giving it, and you may have had some poor experiences receiving it. That's fine, because this fact is the crux of the issue.

Given the organisational cultures and context you have likely grown up in — or are growing up in — feedback is traditionally viewed as something that someone gives to someone else, like an unwanted gift or surprise. A recent article in *Harvard Business Review* makes it clear that giving feedback can have the opposite effect than what's indended. Rather than encouraging development, feedback might actually inhibit growth if given the wrong way.

What if you changed how you view feedback?

Could you see it as something to actively seek rather than something to wait for, secretly cringing when it's imposed upon you?

If you ask for or request feedback, would doing so make it easier to receive it?

It might actually open your mind and heart to what you're about to hear — and to the idea that what's coming is something you want, and even welcome. You could feel good about it, since your intention in requesting it is to learn and grow.

Imagine a world where getting feedback isn't threatening, and asking for it is actually second nature.

Asking for feedback, and being open to receiving and learning from it, makes for some great conversations. How does one do it?

That's where the Plus/Delta technique comes in. I learned it years ago in San Francisco. Developed by Interaction Associates, it continues to serve me, my team, and my clients.

Two sets of questions help spur productive conversations. First, the Plus questions:

- What worked/is working well for you?
- What would you like to do more of because it works?

- What could make this an even better experience for you?

Then the Delta, or learning question:

- What would you change, do differently, upgrade or improve to make this work better for you?

You can also ask yourself:

- What did I do well?
- What might I change or do differently?

What changes when we rethink feedback? Instead of it being a 'burden', can we make it a teaching tool we actively seek?

PRACTICE

Ask the Plus/Delta questions at the end of meetings and conversations.
As a leader, ask team members to give their Plus/Deltas on you.
In the process, you'll help each other grow, learn, and make a difference.

49. LET THE CONVERSATION CHANGE YOU

While I was writing my last book, *Asking Great Questions*, my editor suggested a wonderful book to me: *Conversation: How Talk Can Change Our Lives*, by Theodore Zeldin. Compiled from a series of talks by Zeldin — named one of today's most influential thinkers — it explores the evolution and contribution of conversation in many walks of life.

I was only a few pages in when one phrase stopped me in my tracks. It stays with me:

"The conversation I'm interested in is the one which you start, with a willingness to emerge a slightly different person."

I've discovered this same thing in many years of coaching — that there are conversations from which coach and client emerge as slightly different people.

- We gain new insight about how we show up.
- We discover new possibilities for action.
- We shift our emotional, mental, spiritual and even physical states.
- We're changed because of the space that the conversation created, thanks to practices similar to those in this book.

When I shared this quote with a bright, innovative-thinking leader, however, her first response was, "I don't want to be changed by the conversation." She misinterpreted it as meaning she would be changed by another person's ideas. She wanted to hang on to her own.

Many leaders believe it is their role to change others by imposing or arguing their side of the story.

All too often, this belief is the very block that prevents great conversation — the type that might lead to growth, innovation, creativity, discovery and breakthroughs — from happening.

It's the conversation space itself that has the potential to change you if you are open to it:

- When you meet another person in the space of pure curiosity, with a belief that something is possible beyond what you both know or have experienced to date...
- When you listen for what you haven't heard before...
- When you let go of your need to be right, and consider all perspectives...

- When you start from the possibility that everyone holds some part of the truth...
- When you ask questions that you genuinely don't know the answer to...
- And when you listen for what's ready to emerge...

That's when the conversation will reveal more of who you are, and of what's possible.

You just might find yourself changed by it.

PRACTICE

Be willing to learn something new in every conversation. Hear something you haven't heard before. Be more aware of yourself and others. Listen for what wants to emerge.

IN CLOSING

This book has been a long time in the making. I first had the idea for it in late 2016. By early 2018, I had rough outlines for each chapter. Yet it still didn't want to come to life. It needed something more.

In late 2018 I hired my editor, Dave Jarecki to at last bring the focus and discipline to get it done. I realised it was not for me to struggle with on my own and — true to form — when I brought someone else 'into the conversation', we started to turn it around together. The book took shape.

On the face of it, this book shouldn't have taken this long to be birthed. It was more a question of what purpose it served. Would it be useful? Was it needed? Would it help people?

I had lots of questions about it, despite the fact that I'd been holding conversations for more than 20 years where these same themes kept showing up. Time and again, I'd see the difference a great conversation made for clients when they found subtle, yet impactful shifts in how they were talking to themselves and with others.

Then, just as *The Conversation Edge* was getting close to being ready, I found what I now believe to be a very meaningful purpose for the role conversation plays in our future. A workshop at the Findhorn Foundation called "Peace in Action" by Dr. Scilla Elworthy caught my eye.

Dr. Elworthy, nominated three times for the Nobel Peace Prize, creates and leads dialogue between nuclear weapons policy makers and their critics worldwide. She is an ambassador for sustainable world peace. In her book, *The Business Plan for Peace*, she challenges the global arms race, and awakens leaders and governments with her compelling case for momentous and meaningful world change.

Compared to her life's work, my own world seems comparatively small. I hesitate to presume I'd have the passion, drive or commitment that Dr. Elworthy has to tackle such big, world-changing causes.[16]

I was approaching the end of Dr. Elworthy's book when I stopped at her list of 'useful tools'. And I caught my breath.

Dr. Elworthy and her colleague, Liz Kingsnorth, cite 10 tools for effective communication. Instantly, I saw significant similarities between their tools, and the practices I had been pulling together:

1. An intention for connection (practices 1-9)
2. Listen more than you speak (practices 4, 5, 21, 22)
3. Understand the other person first (practices 6, 15, 34)
4. Understand needs, wishes and values (practices 13, 14, 18, 33)
5. Begin with empathy (practices 16, 35)
6. Take responsibility for your feelings (practices 13, 15, 27, 43)
7. Make requests that are practical, specific and positive (practices 7, 24, 39, 48)
8. Use accurate, neutral descriptions (practices 5, 6, 11, 12, 15)
9. Be willing to hear NO (practices 17, 36, 39, 49)
10. Communicate with more than words (practices 3, 20, 21, 22, 30)

There was more. Their tools for creating better meetings, transforming conflict, and learning to listen more deeply echoed elements of conversation I touch upon between these covers.

I felt butterflies jitter in my stomach. I grabbed her book and headed off for coffee with a friend. We had barely sat down over our lattes before I was pushing Dr. Elworthy's book under his nose.

"Look at the amazing work this woman has done with her life. I'm really inspired by her." I began to relate stories from the book with him.

"It's about connection, and listening, and slowing down, and pausing, and hearing each other, and being empathic, and asking questions, and…and…and… it's about the work I've been doing for years," I exclaimed.

Suddenly, it was clear to me. *The Conversation Edge* does serve a purpose in the world — one that may be bigger than any of us. To quote Dr. Elworthy:

> "The new brand of leaders that we need — those who are actually able to meet the challenges of today and thrive in the world of tomorrow — are the ones who know and live the connection between inner self-development and outer action.

"If we want to communicate clearly, transform conflicts, generate energy and develop trust within our families and in our places of work, our first challenge is to do our inner work. This is the current evolutionary challenge that most people don't yet grasp: that the desired outer changes cannot come about without the inner change."

My years of coaching have revealed that inner change happens one conversation at a time, at those edges that invite us to stretch, become more self-aware, to take risks and open to new possibilities.

My world travels may not have taken me to war zones. I may not have witnessed first hand the harrowing scars of deprived citizens and starving children, or walked alongside armed troops into danger, as Dr. Elworthy has. In my own way, however, I have witnessed edges:

- In conversation with people from 23 different nationalities together in one room.
- In the eyes of a Kazakh national when we didn't speak each other's language and yet could hear what the other wanted to convey.
- In the tears of a young Arab office boy when he felt seen, heard and respected by his higher-ranking managers, for the first time.
- In the personal transformation of strong-minded corporate leaders when they drop their professional shield and show up more fully, connecting with others, person-to-person.

And from conversations I have every day, I witness small steps for personal, organisational and community change.

It is in these conversation spaces, and at these personal edges, that the practices in this book will serve to create more peaceful, sustainable and inspiring possibilities in you and everyone you converse with.

I said at the start of this book that enriching your conversations might enrich your life. How much greater will the impact be if, with deeper conversations, we save not only ourselves, but others too.

It starts with each of us, and in every conversation.

It has to be worth a great conversation.

I wish you many,

Aileen

"How can we have better and more fruitful conversations? I see conversation being the only tool, short of violence, that we have, to get major change happening in the world."[17]

— SAM HARRIS

ACKNOWLEDGEMENTS

First and foremost, my grateful thanks to the many clients and colleagues with whom I have shared inspiring and insightful conversations over the years. You may find traces of our conversations in one or more of the vignettes in this book, identities changed of course, to respect your individuality. Thank you for allowing your story to translate into what I hope will be valuable learning for a wider audience. At the end of the day, our human stories often share the same essence, albeit our circumstances and contexts vary with time and place.

Thank you to my amazing editor, Dave Jarecki, who took my sometimes careless writing to another level with supreme attention to detail. I appreciate how you kept 'my voice' in the writing at the same time as elevating it, Dave. Your skills are amazing.

Once again, my thanks to Lieve Maas, for both the cover and internal design of this book. You totally 'got me' again, Lieve, and I am grateful for the beauty, simplicity and impact this book will have as it goes out into the world. Deepest thanks.

Thank you to friends, family and colleagues for reading the pre-production draft, and for your quotes and endorsements.

Untold thanks to the conversations themselves. Who knew how much power the conversation space offers to transform people's lives? Both simple and profound at the same time.

Finally, I have done my best to correctly attribute the sources and references used throughout this book. It's difficult sometimes to know original sources, given how information is shared and re-shared online.

Any errors in this respect are unintentional. I would be grateful if you would inform me directly if anything seems inappropriately attributed or cited, so I may ensure its correction. Thank you.

ABOUT THE AUTHOR

Aileen Gibb inspires conversations with interesting people and mission-driven businesses, in order to re-shape life and transform leadership. She asks the questions you might not be asking yourself — questions that shift everything, and take your life and business from good to great. And she hears what you're not hearing for yourself. She works with leaders internationally, whilst spending time in both her Scottish homeland and her adopted home in the Rocky Mountains of Alberta, Canada. Her book, *Asking Great Questions,* is described as an essential companion for every leader and is available on Amazon. Aileen can be contacted at www.aileengibb.com and on social media. Email Aileen at aileengibb@icloud.com to explore working with her.

NOTES

I'm grateful to all of the amazingly insightful and creative people whose work continues to influence me. Below is a rundown of the various footnotes you may have noticed throughout the book, along with the corresponding page numbers for reference:

1. From the Foreword, vii: Heard during the *On Being* podcast, in reference to the work of Jennifer S. Temel, MD, at Massachusetts General Hospital; https://onbeing.org/programs/atul-gawande-what-matters-in-the-end/

2. From the Introduction, xvii: This is an excerpt from Cameron's wonderful poem, "We Need a New Map." You can read it in its entirety at http://sandycameron.vcn.bc.ca/2012/we-need-a-new-map/.

3. Page 31: Zak's article appears in the January/February 2017 issue of *Harvard Business Review*, online at https://hbr.org/2017/01/the-neuroscience-of-trust

4. Page 40: This comes from the *Manage Smarter!* podcast #19, "Tom Peters, the Excellence Dividend"; http://salesfuel.com/manage-smarter-19-tom-peters-excellence-dividend/

5. Page 44: Watch the "four candles/fork handles" sketch here if you haven't seen it: http://www.youtube.com/watch?w=gi_6SaqVQSw

6. Page 48: *Making Sense* podcast #142, "Addiction, Depression, and a Meaningful Life" (with Johann Hari); https://samharris.org/podcasts/142-addiction-depression-meaningful-life/

7. Page 53: This short clip of Sinek is less than two-minutes long, and well worth it if you have time to spare: https://www.youtube.com/watch?v=IP_UbJu7xwE

8. Page 60: This wonderful quote comes from Wilber's book, *A Theory of Everything*, published in 2000 by Shambhala.

9. Page 62: The quote seems to paraphrase Dale Carnegie, who wrote in *How to Win Friends and Influence People*, "To be interesting, be interested." https://www.goodreads.com/quotes/868021-to-be-interesting-be-interested

10. Page 64: This quote has been attributed at different times to Henry Ford, Jessie Potter, Tony Robbins and others. The website, QuoteInvestigator.com, leaves the answer open to interpretation. It's a wonderful quote, regardless of its origin.

See: https://quoteinvestigator.com/category/jessie-potter/

11. Page 68: There are many examples of Appreciative Inquiry online. This entry from Positive Psychology makes a nice introduction to the concept: https://positivepsychology.com/appreciative-inquiry/

12. Page 71: The quote comes from an interview with business journalist, Suzy Welch. https://www.linkedin.com/pulse/thrive-under-armour-you-have-answer-kevin-planks-three-suzy-welch/

13. Page 112: Learn more about the WE Institute online: http://www.creatingwe.com

14. Page 128: You can watch it here, if you are so inclined: https://www.youtube.com/watch?v=S0J-RzzzXls

15. Page 130: The song was written by Michael Brown, Bob Calilli, and Tony Sansone, for the band, The Left Banke. The track was released as a single in July 1966. I wonder how many other people mis-hear the lyrics?

16. Page 143: If you don't know her work, you can start by visiting her website: https://www.scillaelworthy.com

17. Page 147: The last quote in the book comes from the *Making Sense* podcast, #119, "Hidden Motives," March 2018; https://samharris.org/podcasts/119-hidden-motives/

Made in the USA
Columbia, SC
10 February 2020

87765797R00085